# Praise for
## *Dear Mama in the Darkness*

"*Dear Mama* is so inspiring, so heartbreaking, so touching, so real and so needed! I sobbed with heartbreak, hope and joy. Hilary shares her soul with compassion, empathy and humor to comfort parents in pain – to let them know that they – that *we* – are not alone."

— Brenda Chapman – Mama, Writer/Director and Academy Award Winner of Disney/Pixar's *Brave*

"A powerful, inspiring, perspective for dads, moms, and really anyone on the sidelines."

— Luther Elliss, Dad to a Medically-Fragile Kiddo, Coach, Former All-American NFL Player

"Providers would do well to read these passages filled with wisdom, humor, humility, and hope to understand how our own training affects us and how that affects our patients and parents. Perhaps this awareness alone can create a revolution in trauma informed care and buck the current systems and approaches."

— Dianna Yip, DO, Pediatric Palliative Care, Dell Children's Medical Center, Mind Body Medicine, Moon Rabbit Medicine

"Beautiful. Hilary has a way of writing what is in my heart."

— Amber Blomquist, Heart Transplant Mama, COO StageDotO Ventures

# DEAR MAMA
## IN THE
# DARKNESS

# DEAR MAMA
## IN THE
# DARKNESS

### WORDS OF ENCOURAGEMENT TO LIGHT THE WAY FOR PARENTS OF MEDICALLY COMPLEX CHILDREN

## HILARY CAMILLE THOMPSON, CLC

THIN LEAF PRESS | LOS ANGELES

Library of Congress Cataloging-in-Publication Data
Names: Thompson, Hilary Camille, Author
Title: *Dear Mama in the Darkness*
LCCN: 2024906081

ISBN 978-1-953183-50-7 (hardcover)
ISBN 978-1-953183-53-8 (paperback)
ISBN 978-1-953183-49-1 (eBook)

Non-Fiction, Parenting, Trauma, Inspirational
Front Photo by Sue Smart Photography 2013
Book Cover Design and Interior Formatting by 100Covers.
Thin Leaf Press | Los Angeles

# Table of Contents

To my partner in the foxhole, my comic relief, scaffolding, and best friend since 1997–I love the story of us. To my incredible girls who made me fearless and proud, and who showed me who I was created to be, and who love me despite my flaws. To my mother, our "Mimi" who was the original cheerleader. To Silas for life. And to everyone who came out of the woodwork when life got hard—you know who you are–thank you.

And to everyone who wants to help someone with a sick kiddo—just show up. Don't ask, just show up. Bonus points if you show up carrying this book and a latte.

# About the Author

Hilary Camille Thompson, CLC, is a lot of things, but it is the title of "Mama" that she treasures most. She is a certified life coach specializing in better mental health, using methods such as inquiry-based stress relief (IBSR) and cognitive behavioral therapy (CBT). She is an international best-selling author, and an accomplished speaker, teacher and mental health practitioner. She specializes in teaching tools to individuals and teams that lend in healing trauma, anxiety and depression, and radically improving life quality.

Hilary grew up in an urban community in Utah, writing stories as soon as she could hold a pencil. Her path has been just a little rocky, but it fueled a desperate desire to become *better* not *bitter*. "I'll figure it out" became a favorite phrase.

The real revolution, though, began in 2011, when Hilary gave birth to a small miracle—the catalyst for sharing her way while climbing a seemingly insurmountable path—baby on her hip. It was a rough and winding road, but she was intent on smoothing the way for others walking behind her. She believes strongly in empowering people to find their own way to wholeness, and realize their potential, their worth, and the beauty in their struggle. Founding HARTT Mental Health Coaching in 2020 brought that dream to fruition.

In 2022, Hilary moved to the country with her family to build their sammeltasse chicken collection and find peace, fresh air, and the Country Wave. She works tirelessly to advocate for kids with medical trauma, educating providers and coaching parents, and works with clients and corporations across the country in her practice as an online mental health coach.

Dear Mama in the Darkness is a collection of letters she wrote to document the revolution that took place between 2011 - 2023. A dozen years of creating her kintsugi. On her headstone, it will likely say "She figured it out. Coffee helped a lot."

Works in Progress:

*The Road to Healing Childhood Medical Trauma* (working title) A brief guide for parents and providers.

*Illuminating Grief & Trauma* (working title) an incredibly effective, sacred, and personalized method to find your way when walking through the healing process of trauma and grief.

# Introduction

Have you heard of "kintsugi?" It's the Japanese art of filling the cracks of broken pottery with gold. With this, the Japanese take an otherwise broken and useless bowl, for example, and they turn it into something beautiful. They use these imperfections that would otherwise render something as damaged beyond repair, to create something so much better. Stronger. Even precious. As a parent of a medically complex child, we also have the ability to let our cracks define us, or to make our "broken," beautiful.

First crack: "There's something wrong with your child."

Second crack, third crack, one thousand seven hundred twenty-third crack to follow. This wasn't what you pictured parenting would look like. If you've received the news that your child is unwell, the range of emotions is as unique as the parent, from merely unsettling to absolutely devastating. Often we triumph, heal, and persevere, but at times it can feel like you are lost, trying to reassemble you and your child's lives without a lantern. Darkness.

You might not have time to grieve, you may just have to get through the next moment, and the next. And somehow, when catching a glimpse of your bedraggled image in a mirror, you realize that you are the adult here. Crack.

You may feel a bit lost, in the dark. Or maybe that was you two, five, or seven years ago. Maybe the darkness only comes occasionally these days. That is why I've titled this book as "Dear Mama in the Darkness," (they were letters originally written to myself) but you don't have to be a "Mama" to appreciate it, and you don't have to remain in the dark...I brought a lantern.

Consider this book a hot flow of golden words; your healing salve, your CPR, that 247th wind you need. Chicken soup for the weary soul. Filling your bucket will bless your child too. Read it in the glow of the machines, read it at the bedside, read it celebrating another day where you landed on your feet, miraculously upright and still breathing.

If there's one thing you have, it's perspective, and if you're reading this, odds are you want to be better, not bitter. Or maybe you're just searching for compassion, a sisterhood in the darkness. The following pages are lessons, thoughts, letters to myself, from the road I walked before you on this journey.

A wise soul once told me that parenting a medically complex child is a marathon, not a sprint. I hope these pages become worn and tattered with your turning, and crinkled with the tears you shed, watery witnesses to your healing journey.

I hope this blesses your cracks with gold, you tattered warrior. Let the gold shimmer and light your way.

Signed,

Your fearless cheerleader

"I said: what about my eyes?
He said: Keep them on the road.
I said: What about my passion?
He said: Keep it burning.
I said: What about my heart?
He said: Tell me what you hold
inside it? I said: Pain and sorrow.
He said: Stay with it. The wound is
the place where the Light
enters you."

— **Rumi**

The morning of Shiloh's 3rd open-heart surgery in Boston, 2013

"Parenting a complex child is often more about surviving than *thriving*. But wouldn't it be neat if we could do BOTH?"

# Chapter 1

# CPR AND A HIGH-FIVE FROM YOUR TATTERED CHEERLEADER

People ask me what I've learned from my journey through diagnosis, complications, surgeries, balancing a full life with other obligations, two kids (that feel like six), a job, a marriage, fighting for my child to live, surrendering, getting back up onto that horse, trying to become better, not bitter, adapting to a "new normal" and trying to make that "normal" a life we enjoy, not just endure…it's been an exhausting journey that many can relate to. So, oh, boy, that's a big question: what have I learned? So many lessons, and most of them are contained within this book. I wrote my way through healing my own trauma and my kiddo's too. It was one of the dozens of tools I picked up while trudging this road.

I learned that many of us, including me, felt broken; damaged. I also knew I didn't like the feeling. But I *was* changed beyond recognition. How could I find joy in this…wreckage? The tools I picked up remind me of kintsugi. Taking broken pieces of pottery, reassembling them with golden scars. Some of us, in fact, most of us, are just trying to pick up our broken pieces and awkwardly carry them, feeling even more burdened, but hoping one day for repair. Some of us are actually trying to make something beautiful from the brokenness by finding purpose in it. Finding the lessons, the reasons, in it.

One of the biggest lessons I've learned is to show up. To lift up. That there is no comparing one parent's journey to another, and that part of the blessing of this journey is to share things we've learned in order to make this path a smidgen easier for those walking behind us. I read once that we're all just walking each other home.

While you're climbing that mountain, be sure to look back and see how far you've come. See the gold that's filling in some of your cracks. Notice it in your child's scars, too. You're stronger than you think you are, and so are they.

## Take Heart, Warrior

Hey you, warrior. Do you know just how amazing you are? Do you have a moment to stand back and comprehend it with me?

Your battlecry is "anything for my child." You've stood in circles of doctors with degrees longer than your arms and defended your gut feeling. You've watched a monitor with your child's future on it for days, weeks, months. You've felt the sternal wires holding your child's chest together when you rocked her at night. You've set alarms for meds and you've shamed yourself for being five minutes late with them. You've read and re-read that diagnosis, you've walked the halls with an IV pole in one hand and a sick child in another. You've prayed for good X-rays, labs, biopsies and surgeries. You've prayed for no more surgeries and lost. Sometimes on your knees, sometimes in the waiting room, maybe even just this moment, you've begged for your child's life. You've fought the insurance company seven times for the same bill at a time when you should've been by her side. You paid them however you could, and you've stood helpless when they wouldn't pay for your last hope for treatment. You've had all the eggs in that basket break. You've been crushed upon the two rocks of Hope and Desperation.

But here's the thing: you're reading this, which means you're still breathing. You have survived the raging storm and what is more, you carried a sick child with you the whole way. Forget the Ironman. This is what makes a hero.

Don't let it break you. Can't breathe? Consider this love note from me your CPR. You can choose to be better or be bitter. The choice is really yours—we are not victims. We are warriors CHOSEN for battle. Let this fight be your love song. Let your joy be that much more joyous because you have known such pain. You have a perspective that no one else has. You know how precious life is, don't you?

I hope you know how precious you are, warrior. Keep fighting.

## Keep Pressing, Mama.

When you found out that the child you love was "broken," you were given several options. You chose to fight for both of you. You had no idea what kind of battle you were signing up for. You've made all kinds of life and death choices since, you've sat on the frontlines of the ICU, machines beeping their battle march. You've surrendered to the least-bad decision. You've said goodbye a lot. You've waited a lot. You've advocated yourself silly.

Each day calls again, "Be brave, Mama. She needs you to be."

"Be brave because she has to be."

And, fueled by coffee, spirit, a little bit of attitude, and a lot of chutzpah, you rise again. Sometimes it takes putting on your big girl pants and getting that 367th wind. Again.

And some days you don't win.

But being brave means you keep showing up. You rise again like a freaking Phoenix from its ashes, give yourself a hug and a high five and do it again. And again. And again. And again.

Because you're not climbing a mountain. You are trekking the whole darn range. It's exhausting, but each time you reach another summit, you can hold each other tight and say, "We did it."

Again, and again, and again.

Keep pressing, Mama.

Finding peace, rocking Shiloh beofre her transplant, October 2013

## A Change of Heart (Be Brave, Mama)

Have you ever been on the edge of something so big, it swallowed you just thinking about it? Been so used to the devil you know, the sickness, the sadness, the yuck, that even the cure seemed scarier? This room you've been living in is a war zone, but you don't know what's on the other side of the door? Could the hallway be worse? The thought of change leaves you paralyzed.

Getting help for anything feels that way sometimes.

I've faced defeat, lugged oxygen everywhere, sat in the hospital endlessly, worried nights, looked death in the eye, begged for my child's life, but even the thought of being free of that felt... scary? Uncertain. The unknown.

There I was, in the hospital room, rocking my sleeping child on the edge of something new and unknown. The heart that was inside my baby, had given its best effort, had been through so, so much. It was a warrior heart, and it was tired. When I learned that they had found a donor for my daughter, it's hard to describe the emotions. I felt a loving grief for her sick little heart even though it had caused so much pain for all of us. A gratitude.

In that short morning, I went through all the emotions for the donor family, shock, fear, sadness, loss, disbelief, relief, pure exhaustion. Then I just held my baby. I had spent a year prior doing my own therapeutic work to prepare for this moment. Because I did, it didn't take long to see things differently. And as she drifted off, surrendering to sleep, always my teacher, I surrendered. I didn't know what this new chapter would bring. But I was ready. I said goodbye to that room we had spent two years in, and I walked through the door. I signed the surgeon's papers.

There we were, in the hallway between two rooms, in that rocking chair, in limbo, just surrendering to God's will. In limbo, but in peace for what was next:

A change of heart.

What room are you scared to leave? What devil do you know too well? What comfortable pain are you afraid to let go of? Who are you afraid of becoming?

Facing an addiction, quitting that job, leaving abuse, healing trauma, overcoming depression, it is all surgery. It takes bravery and willingness and surrender. Leaving that room, no matter how hard it's been can be scary.

I won't lie and tell you that the next room we entered was perfect. It was different—and better in many ways. There were challenges we didn't expect. Lots of adjustment and learning. What I know is that we don't regret being brave. I'm grateful for the surrender I chose on this beautiful evening in 2013. Grateful I took time to say goodbye and thank you to our old life, our old hearts. Grateful I stepped through that doorway.

I hope you give yourself the chance to visit another room. The view can be breathtaking.

Rocking Shiloh the day before her 3rd surgery in Boston, 2013

"Stay in the moment, Mama. It's all you've ever had this whole time."

## Dear Mama in the Darkness

Hey you, hovering over your child in the dark, hand on her chest, waiting for signs of life. She's there, still breathing. It's your turn.

You, who has scrubbed chest tube juice out of newborn clothes; you, who has held your flailing child while they found a vein; you, who stays up late to check lab results online. You know just enough to be dangerous—just enough to worry. You, who has paced hospital halls, fought the insurance company for the eighth time about the same bill. You, who has sold something you love to pay for it. You, who has wondered if they'll ever walk with that oxygen tube trailing from them, anchored to a foreign machine that sounds like a Harley in your living room. You, who has said goodbye outside the OR more times than you'd like to count. Hey, warrior? What makes you question what you've given her? She's forged from steel, proofed in the fire—just like you.

That frail little bird? She's stronger than you think. She is a survivor. She is made to fight this battle. She is made from a piece of you. Continue to show her how to fight. Continue to hold her hand. She needs it less than you think. Do it anyway. And that future you lie awake at night thinking about? Will she ever fall in love? Go to prom? Graduate college?

That is not now. Now you are missing the soft tendrils of hair against your cheek as you feel her breathing body beside you there in the darkness. Stay in the moment, Mama. It's all you've ever had this whole time.

Breathe.

## We Strong.

News flies past me from many sources lately as I stay within the comfort of my clorox-wiped home, staying dozens of feet from society (because six is not enough). Inundated at times by fear for the fragile girl who has not left our home for days now. Fear because she is the center of the Venn diagram of people who die from this virus I've only read about. "She is so fragile," I think, as I wonder about all the ways the world has changed for us, "We are so fragile."

But is that really true?

Was she not forged in the same fire I'm made of, the steel that wakes in the night to check hospital equipment, flush PICC lines, watch the beeping on a box that holds a child's life, who put it all on the line, who has begged for a miracle and picked up the pieces when it didn't come, who stands shoulder-to-shoulder with doctors day in and day out, who fights for less radiation, more sunshine, chickens, who, in the face of the unknown, chose to say yes to one little life, and one big fight?

I am not fragile.

And she, who has had her ribs carved open four times, who has had machines do the work of her heart, who has fought like a tiger for every moment of sun, who screamed the fiercest battle cry, only moments from my womb, who braved the world with half a heart and exchanged it for another, who walks, willingly to the lab, and knows when to hold a hand, and when to brave it alone, who holds the wisdom of a sassy little old lady, and the daring of someone who doesn't understand time or limits, or worry, or sickness.

She is not fragile.

So in this moment, in this safety of our home that was built on sheer grit, and much love, I will not fear. I will bask in the precious gratitude that only a parent who has held their dying child knows: let her play. Let her swing on that swing that was never promised. Let her enjoy this classroom-free time with her sister, let her fall off her bicycle and get back up. Let her be protected, not because she wants it, but because hospitals don't have swings and she has earned this life outside its walls. Let her see joy in my face—not fear. We brave.

Because God sees us here. He told this story long ago of strength that emerges from hardship. We are made stronger FOR this, THROUGH this, BY this...we are not fragile.

We strong.

## You Have It in You Again.

Even in your darkest moment, you've been okay. On your knees, in grief, prayer, or surrender, the ground held you. Feel the breath in your lungs. Your heart still beats. You have come this far and the universe, God, has always supported you through it—given you what you need. You have been made a warrior, well equipped for battle.

What makes this time any different?

"You've earned this weirdness and every gray hair that sits on your beautiful head."

## When Normal Is Weird

You disappeared into "normal," and it was weird. For so many years, you had life bombs going off constantly, hospitals, PICC lines, IVs, lab draws, meds, oh so many meds, 11PM ER trips, praying for one little girl's life, begging...a lot of all that.

It seems like you got through it okay in the moment, sure you were stressed, but you were surviving. You had no choice.

And when you got through your first year of battle, it's like life threw on an emergency break going full speed. Suddenly the trauma, the anxiety...raging monsters that needed feeding...were ever-present. So there was that to deal with: your own damage. The survey, the repair.

Well, now you're working full time at a job you love. You have a kindergartener and a third grader. Gymnastics, piano, singing lessons for your heart baby, date nights with friends. Life seems...dare you say it...normal. But you're always waiting for something.

The other shoe to drop.

It takes so much effort to stay in the moment, but oh, so worth it when you do. Shouldn't you be enjoying this freedom? This bliss? But yet it always feels like the calm before the storm.

Sing in the rain, Mama. Enjoy the calm. Take pictures, then put away your phone, do what you can do. Because storms do damage, and that spot in you is tender. It's okay for "normal" to feel weird, but you should also enjoy the wind in your hair, and watching your child running free of oxygen tubing.

That is Now.

You've earned this weirdness and every gray hair that sits on your beautiful head. Bask in the glory of you (she's a miracle and she's happy), and stay in the moment. It's all we really have anyway.

## Beating the Heavy: A Pep Talk

I'm sure as a teenager, my step had more of a spring in it. I say this not because I'm almost 40, but because life has dealt me some heavy blows. They weigh me down at the most inconvenient times: the impending doom that casts a shadow on sacredly sweet moments with my four-year old. It alters my vision, so I only see her second heart—her vulnerability in this world in those moments. I have to force it out, like the dark rain clouds that threaten to break over the earth today, over this little city in which I'm stranded.

It takes skill and strength to push out the Heavy.

It takes a lot of running. And a lot of coffee. And a text from a good friend. And a heart mom offering shelter when your car is broken down. And a picture on Facebook of a sweet girl celebrating her 18th year post-heart-transplant. And two little girls that have no idea that death is lurking so they just play Uno on the floor of our little borrowed shelter.

Put on your cheerleader outfit, Hilary. Lace up those sneakers. The world is still beautiful out there. People are celebrating someone's first birthday and someone's 91st birthday today. Gardens are being planted. Magnolias are in bloom. Ignore the storm cloud and make your own light. You've survived that which should have killed you, only about 20 times now. It gave you muscles. Step out into the light—exercise them. You've got friends who send you chocolate in the mail, for crying out loud. You've got a charmed life—it's just a matter of perspective.

Lighten your load and put away the heavy. Or you'll miss the miracle, Hilary. It's right under your nose.

"A message from my past self
to my future self? I think so."

## Make Your Own Fun Cup

I was labeling plastic cups at a family barbecue with a sharpie. And yes, of course, you know me; instead of their real names, I was making up and scribbling silly nicknames (I mean, duh.) Each niece and nephew filed in, excited to see each other's "Fun Cup." Blewberry and GiggleBritches asked me if they could make me my own Fun Cup, which sparked an idea. I said "no."

I stopped what I was doing and I looked at them seriously. Trying to really drive home my point, I said to them, "Aunt Hilly makes her OWN Fun Cup. If there is ever one thing that this Silly Aunt of yours could teach you girls, (who were admittedly towering over me having a terribly difficult time taking me as seriously as I wanted them to) it is this:

> You only really have you.
> Make your own Fun Cup.
> Throw your own party.
> Don't wait for the world to do it for you.

Flash forward to two weeks later. I was to relearn my own lesson.

As I scrolled through seemingly endless European selfies on Facebook (and I don't mean the nude kind although that would have been shocking coming from my particular friend list) I wiped an envious tear from my eye. For some reason that week, every single person I knew had gone to Europe. London, Italy, Switzerland, France. I'm serious—it's as if they were just highlighting step-by-step everything I was missing on this Earth. I fought the urge to weep openly.

Just then, a picture text flashed on my phone. It was GiggleBritches'. She had created a meme for her cell phone picture cover. What did it say? "Make your own fun cup."

I glanced over at my medically-fragile daughter. It practically required a medical degree to care for her. Forget a babysitter,

I needed a hospital staff. Outside the rains drenched every hope I had of going to Europe with my husband—thousands of miles away from my daughter's carefully managed array of medical supplies, appointments, medication lists, and weekly lab work. I glanced back at my phone. "Make Your Own Fun Cup," it said. A message from my past self to my future self? I think so.

Instead of Hilary Camille Thompson going to Italy this summer, Italy came to her. A couple trips to a couple stores and some elbow grease, and "Voila!" Only you know what's even better about MY fun cup? My Italy stays here. All. Summer. Long.

Well friends, I must run along. Time to plan my blockbuster of a 40th birthday party. I know it's a year away, but some Fun Cups take some serious leg work.

Get back on that (rocking) horse.

## Get Back on That Horse

Perseverance—it's what makes America, well, America. Forget that; it's what makes humans human. We get picked on, stepped on, shut down, and we just get back up. The scale of humanity's ability to keep on keepin' on is monumental.

Everyone has a survivor story. I lift you up with mine; you keep me going with yours. Sometimes the road is paved with gold and we slide, slick-heeled to the finish line. Other times, we pull each other along in a slow, steady, grunting, trudge uphill knee-deep in tar. For most, it is a mixture of these two extremes.

After months of the disheartening trickling-in of rejection letters from the literary agents I've chosen to grace with my heart-song (an earlier version of the book you are reading)I got back on that horse. I put my fingers to the keys and sent out my manuscript to four more agents today. Sometimes life is about shouting in the face of naysayers, "I will not back down!" My book is not going to publish itself, and it is similar to sifting through the sands of the river to find the golden nugget of representation I seek: it is a tireless act of dedication and perseverance. I know that my manuscript will find itself perched between the right set of hands sooner than later. I have a dream. And a long list of agents.

I have a lifetime of getting back on that horse. So do you, I hope. So good to exercise our heart muscles and keep trying. In my case, I learned from the very best. Here's to the sliding and the trudging together.

"My daughter and I are not victims of circumstance. We are survivors."

## Love, Hearts, and Other Bloody Truths

I threw a pity party the other day, it was short-lived but it was indeed pitiful. The thought, "Why us?" played its soundtrack on repeat. Me, born with a disease that has damaged my body, and my sweet baby girl, four years old and on her second heart. The truth is, I'll never know why. And it really would make no difference if I did. What does make a difference is the CHOICE I make to see things in a better light, no matter what.

My daughter and I are not victims of circumstance. We are survivors.

The sourness of the lemons we've been handed makes ordinary life so much sweeter. Every jelly soaked hand-hold, every push on the swing, every "Mom" scribbled in washable marker, bears witness to our love in that moment. The real truth is, I feel giddy with luckiness most days. My girls have no idea how debilitating my disease can get, so I take their lead and act as if the future is limitless. I can be ignorantly blissful if I don't live in the future. The future is suffering, and fear. The future is where many a pity party is held. If I want peace, I live in the now. I have always had exactly what I needed in the moment, if I think about it. I am surrounded by love—everyone is, but not everyone chooses to see it.

May you be blessed by your lemons this Valentine's Day. Share that lemonade generously.

## Rise Again, Warrior.

Whatever you're seeking, it's in you. I've been around long enough to make the mistake of thinking I know what you need. But I do believe in your ability to find it. Only you know the source of your strength– where you've been, what you've conquered, what you've endured. Look within, and harness that same power again. It's time to get your 237th wind, Mama. You're what you've been waiting for this whole time. You can do this.

*Rainbow Dash and Super Girl, Halloween 2012*

## Put on the Cape

Today I stood up for my child. And that is not an ordinary thing. To face anyone—school officials, men and women with medical degrees, another parent, it takes courage.

I made a commitment to a tiny little outline of a baby during our first fetal echocardiogram, to always be there; to always fight for her. When they offered to terminate my pregnancy, or deliver her and take her home to die, I put my hand over my stomach protectively and said "no." Not because I am pro-life, but because I am pro-THIS-life. I loved this child that moved inside of me too much not to fight. Don't get me wrong, surrender is sometimes necessary. Sometimes it is the most peaceful option. But I chose to fight.

Until this little being gives me the indication that the fight is over, then I'm going to do everything in my power to protect her. I've never regretted being her hero, her advocate, her shelter. I'm a walking medical record, I'm a nurse, I'm a physical therapist, I'm a teacher, I'm her sanctuary, I'm the cheerleader she needs.

When I found out about her heart, a wonderful friend sent me a cape and mask. I had no idea then how brave I was really going to have to be.

"You're what you've been
waiting for this whole time.
You can do this."

## The Country Wave

Growing up spending my summers on a ranch in the teeny town of Almo, Idaho, when I wasn't riding horses, turning hay, or shooting BB Guns, my job was to sit on the front porch and whittle. The most important part of that job, though, was to put my hand up solemnly and wave to the rare person driving down our road. I still remember my Dad, the old cowboy's, serious wave. It was his duty. I absolutely felt the honor in it. Stoic.

When I was learning to drive, my parents always told me to wave in my rearview if someone let me in. This used to be common practice. While I grew up just outside of the city, it was still a bigger town, and I'd say most people waved when you let them in. Thirty years later, I still wave. Most people don't. Even kind acts of patiently waiting for people to go in front of me go unrecognized. Truly, I do them just to be kind and shouldn't expect an acknowledgement, but I always try to acknowledge others' kindness if I'm able. Sometimes I tell myself that cars these days have tinted windows—do we see each other as much as we used to? This question runs deep. It seems we've been separated in so many ways.

Then we moved to the country.

Here, everyone waves. If you pass someone walking, you wave. If you pass someone on the quiet road in your car, you wave approximately 10 feet before you pass each other. If you're in your yard and someone drives by, you wave. If there is no wave, there's a strange, empty feeling. I. Love. The. Country. Wave. It says:

"I see you."

"We are both here, living this life, at the same time and the same place."

"We are both in this thing."

"Together, in this moment."

"I'm acknowledging this thing we share."

"Even if it's just the same road."

Why do I love this so much? This feeling of kinship? When I go to the city now, I feel its absence dearly. I feel disconnected and separated. Why is this so important to me? I've spent a lot of time thinking about The Country Wave, and it's so much more than just a wave.

In May of 2013, I was in the hall on the eighth floor of Boston Children's Hospital receiving some very bad news. For those that don't know, the eighth floor is all heart families. Various types of kiddos and conditions, but it is all pediatric cardiology patients and their families.

There, outside my daughter's hospital room, I was learning that her rare and complex heart surgery was failing. There in the hall, my grief must have been physically visible. My body shaking in sobs. Suddenly, and quietly, I felt these soft arms around me. A stranger, a heart mama, just knowing, just hugging me.

"I see you."

"We are both here, living this life, at the same time and the same place."

"We are both in this thing."

"Together, in this moment."

"I'm acknowledging this thing we share."

Even if it's just the same road.

The Country Wave.

When I met her and asked her about it later, she said, "It's just what heart moms do."

Let's all be a little more human together. Yes, there are hundreds of cheesy and honest articles lately begging everyone to "just get along." I'm not asking that. Boundaries are healthy and necessary sometimes. Tolerance can often be enabling unhealthy behavior. Values and views differ. Perceptions and perspectives differ and change. There is a lot going on in the world. Just acknowledge everyone's innate humanity. Find unity in something, even if it's just a heartbeat.

I'm here, you're here, I see you doing your best. It's hard. Look up at the car passing you. Wave. That's it.

And bring back The Country Wave.

## Let Fear Be My Valentine

The opposite of fear is love. But the two can go hand in hand—as you embrace fear, it can become your true love. It tells you where your future lies if you are brave enough to do what you fear most.

I have a picture of the envelope and the unused stamp hovering near it, taken by a friend, on the day I sent my manuscript out into the world. It is intense vulnerability: the distinct possibility of rejection. It is me facing my fear and turning it into love. It is putting the stamp on the letter.

Our time on this Earth is limited. What is your greatest potential? What fear is limiting you? Fear tells us we are alive; love lets us live. What do you have to lose by taking that risk?

Put the stamp on the letter.

## Chapter 2

# I OWN STOCK IN KLEENEX

When we were diagnosed with Shiloh's heart condition, we were remodeling our bathroom (we were about to share it among four people). My husband wanted to stop the work—he didn't want to be in a crisis with workers in the house. I said, "No—I need that bathtub." And boy, did I. I'd come home from the hospital and cry in that tub. Literally bathing in my tears. Today I joke that I've run out of tears as I don't cry very often. But the truth is that I've healed most of the things I'd used to cry about—partly, by crying.

I tell my clients that I offer solutions, the gold, to fill those cracks they've encountered along the way. But there is a time to marinate in the sadness, feel the feelings, experience the losses, soak in the bathtub and let the tears run. And when you are ready to stop the suffering, you can pick up your tools and mend your cracks. It is the dance of grief, and I've come to see my grief a beautiful dedication. I've made peace with it. I look in the mirror, and see the cracks in my visage, and in my mind's eye, they shine with the gold I've laid there. I couldn't have done that without the tears. They are holy.

Fall leaves. Hope, beckoning for more. 2019

"I know that the future will come soon enough, and it will not look like I imagined."

## Dear Hope

I haven't trained you yet to give me the things my heart longs for between pauses in conversation at the park. I hear you calling me when I see my daughter's hair filled with fall leaves under the Sycamore tree...just playing.

You say, "More. I want more of this."

You say, "I want her to grow up, to have growing pains, acne, to be picked last in dodgeball in junior high. I want her mouth to hurt from braces and her sneezing fits during season after season after season of playing in these fall leaves."

"I want her to experience first love, and heartbreak, and I want to get frustrated while I teach her to drive and she burns out my clutch. I want to go through a hundred clutches. I want to wait up for her when she comes home too late. I want to force her through a million pictures at her last prom and I want to see her walk across the stage in a cap and gown and trip, just a little, I want her to look for me in the crowd frantically waving and shooting pictures. I want to help her fill out college applications and wait nervously with her to hear back, praying she'll be close, but her dreams closer. I want to feel that ache as she leaves me for something bigger, and I want that anticipation of her returning. I want her to be a wife and a mother and all the joy and heartache that comes with that. I want to see her get her first gray hair."

Hope, you woke me up in the night, you were with me in traffic on the way home from the hospital, on Instagram as I watched the other mothers celebrate milestones, birthdays, high school dances. I just want that.

Sometimes, Hope, you've held me up on the achiest days of begging on my knees for just another day with her, that small, hot dream of a future. Some days I lost you and wandered in the darkness. I've put way too much on your shoulders.

Today, Hope, you are not my everything. I know that the future will come soon enough, and it will not look like I imagined. Today, Hope, you have been replaced with Now.

Now says, "Be here. Love this. See her. In this moment. Take this in. Don't get all future-y, Mama. She's here. Be Grateful." And if I obey...oh, God, please let my heart obey...this season of fall leaves is enough.

In Gratitude.

## A Letter to an Angel's Mom

In 2013, while we were in the hospital waiting for a heart transplant for my Shiloh (who was then barely less than two), my four-year-old, Juna only knew that Shiloh was sick. When I entered Juna in preschool that fall, I sent a letter to all the parents, humbly asking them to keep kids home when they are really sick, and to please alert us about what would be life-threatening illnesses for Shiloh (things like RSV, chicken pox, flu, etc.) Any illness that Juna brought home to Shiloh could temporarily de-list her. I had good response. What I did not anticipate was one of the kids in the classroom asking Juna if her sister had "gotten her heart yet."

This prompted a much-needed talk. I never want to lie to my children. What I needed was an age-appropriate version of the truth and one that could grow with her as she matured. I told Juna this: "Your little sissy has a very, very sick heart, which is why she is in the hospital. We are waiting for an angel. We are waiting for an angel to bring Shiloh a special heart." This is something that a four-year-old could understand. Every day for quite a while, Juna talked about Shiloh's Angel Heart. This is what our family calls her little heart now.

Shortly after her transplant, I wrote a letter to that Angel's mother. Not that these events and this gift need any more depth and weight for me, but our particular Angel was Juna's age. He would be cutting out snowflakes with his kindergarten class to-day. His family will celebrate his birthday soon, so I sent a letter filled with gratitude. I called him our little savior, and that is not far from the truth. He is the reason we had four stockings on our mantle at Christmas this year.

It's amazing how one relationship, one heart, one yes, one angel, can create such a field of gratitude it leaves one breathless.

"You fought for her, You were her nurse, her playmate, her soldier on the front line. You went above and beyond for that little girl. You gave everything you had. Life is not fair and no one knows what it will bring, but you did your best. You loved."

## To the Mama Saying Goodbye

You've spent a week memorizing her face, holding her little body against you, feeling the weight of her sleeping breath. You've taken pictures and videos. You've played ponies with her and worn a silver crown at the princess ball. You danced. You watched her feather-light hair move in the breeze as you pushed her on the swing. You've read the same book over and over and over again. You kissed her sleeping, watching her chest rise and fall.

Now it's time to say goodbye.

You stand outside of operating room doors and you think to yourself, "What if this is it? What if memories will be all I have left?" You tell yourself that at least they will be good memories—but it doesn't seem enough. You close your eyes and think of her little chubby arms wrapped around your neck. You long to feel that again. Right now.

"She needs to be able to grow up!" Your mind screams as the doors close. Frozen, you realize you have to move, so you make your way to the waiting room to wait two, four, maybe even seven hours. They'll page you when she's done. The pager on your hip they've given you feels like a ticking time bomb.

Here is the thing that should comfort you, Mama: she was loved. If you did nothing else, you loved her. You fought for her, you were her nurse, her playmate, her soldier on the front line. You went above and beyond for that little girl. You gave everything you had. Life is not fair and no one knows what it will bring, but you did your best. You loved.

And that is all you can do. Odds are, she'll be back in your arms again soon. Until then, I'll be waiting in the waiting room with you.

Daddy and Juna on one of a thousand family hikes.

## The Butterfly on My String

Sometimes you have to run. You have to pick up, pack up, get up and get out to somewhere far away from all things medical. Because she has asked to go to the hospital too many times. Because the doctors aren't "making me all better Mommy." Because they can't find a vein anymore. Because we've tried everything. Because she's sad and just plain sick of being sick, and you can't remember any length of sustained happiness on her face for weeks and weeks. Because you want to find and trap that beautiful little smile like a butterfly in your net and tie a string around it. Your desire for that butterfly trumps even finding the cure. You have lost sense.

Your heart is on empty. Your soul echoes, cavernous. You can't hear your heartbeat through that throbbing ache. Your spirit is on crutches and losing ground. You fear it has caught something incurable and degenerative.

You hear this creature calling you. That wild, mysterious, untamable, wet, gritty, soft, cool Nature. Where the only needles are pine. Where the only Lab just passed you on a leash. The only crying is the songbirds from the canopies above your head as you type these words. She sleeps, covered in the dew of the morning after an evening under the stars playing with friends.

A tear slowly makes its course down the washboards of your crow's feet as your heart fills with the knowledge that you did the right thing. Last night, she was just a kid, not more, not less.

How long will the butterfly stay on this string?

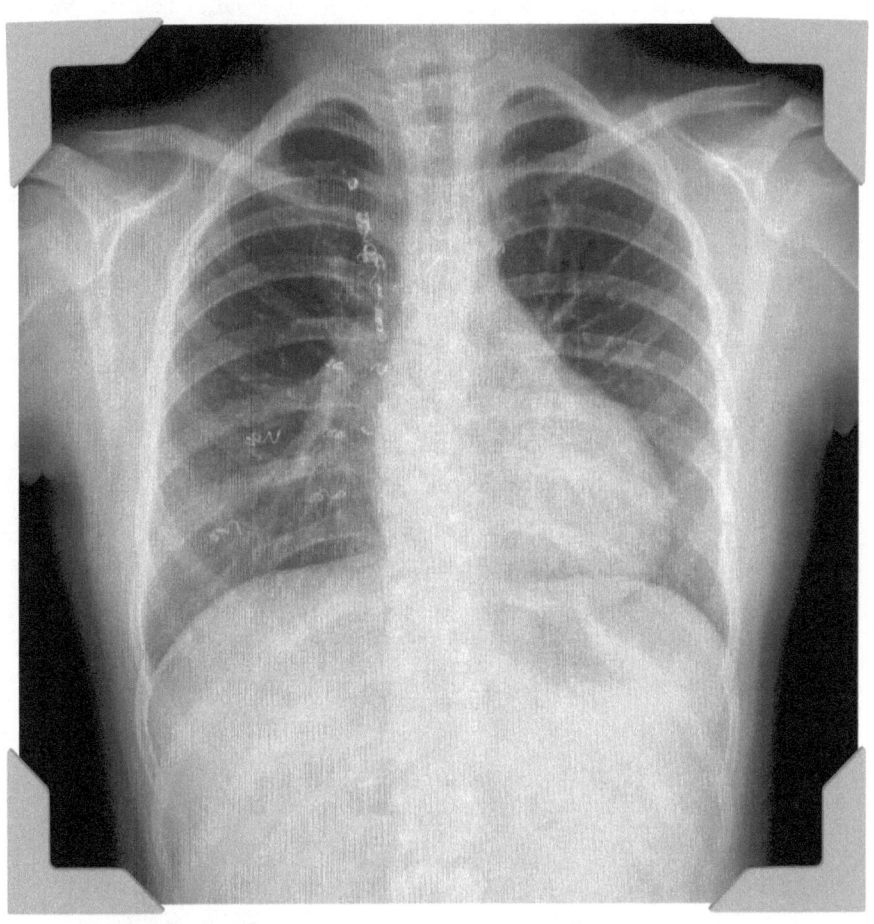

*Window into the heart of a warrior. Silas is in there. So am I. So grateful.*

## A Grateful Heart

Stop and ask a mother about gratitude whose child runs around the playground with another child's heart beating inside them, and you better be prepared to stay awhile. Ask a mother with a chronically ill child, and you'll get the same result. We simply have a different scale by which we measure.

My heart overflows with gratitude. Simply bursting. But it's not always what you'd think—I have a different standard by which to judge. I must.

I'm grateful for the hospital bed that my baby rolled over in for the first time and grateful that other babies roll over on their living room rugs. I'm grateful that the car seat wasn't too small when I finally took my baby home at seven months old, and grateful for babies that come home in two days. I'm grateful for surgeons that visit every day to check on their handiwork when they could be home with their families. I'm grateful for medical science, and also my watchful eyes and gut feeling that have caught a few medical science errors. I'm grateful for that entire year free of anything hospital where my baby got to grow, lose that darn feeding tube, and for a daughter who finally dared to hold her tubeless baby sister. I'm grateful for the courage it took to fly across the country in search of a cure and the humility it took for me to admit it was a dismal failure. I'm grateful for knees that catch me when I fall in grief and desperation. I'm grateful for the prayers of others when I lack any faith of my own. I'm grateful for children's hospitals that cushion all of our falls and Child Life who makes it softer and more fun for my sick child to be tied to her bed with tubes and cords. I'm grateful for family and friends who take shifts at the hospital because I'm so bad at multiplying myself for a sibling.

I am grateful, beyond grateful, soul-shakingly, mind-numbingly grateful for the miracle of organ donation and a family out there in the void who said "yes" on the worst day of their lives. I'm grateful that I can send them letters that contain my poor attempts at expressing monumental gratitude that their little boy's heart is keeping my baby alive, one beat at a time.

And I'm beyond grateful for every day after October 12, 2013, because it is one we came so close to losing. Every swing on the swing, scribble on paper, "Let it Go" sung at the top of her lungs in the back of my car. Every, oh God yes, every day that the soft cushion of her tiny palm presses against mine as we take a walk on fall leaves. Every jelly-soaked kiss on my cheek, every time I gaze on her silvery scar in the bathtub. Every time she hugs her sister when they reunite, and every soft tap on my shoulder waking me at 4 a.m. as I pull her warm body into bed with me. I am grateful for every hug, every breath, every moment at bedtime when her soft snores take over her little chubby body and for the weight that rests on my shoulder. Peaceful.

Gratitude is the sound of that little boy's heart playing a soft beat in the darkness.

"Why? Because love. Hold onto it in the darkness as you lay by your sick child. It is keeping her alive."

## Love Letters

There are two parents whose child is on the other side of the line between Earth and Heaven. They write to me. Their only son's heart, forever four years old, beats in my daughter's chest. I received a letter right before Christmas.

Over the last three years, I have gotten more used to receiving these letters from the people who saved a PERFECT STRANGER with one word, whispered in grief, Yes. I have not gotten used to the circumstances that created our relationship, so messy, so complicated. Our bond, a perfect tangle of grief, desperation, hope, salvation, grace, illness, joy, death, and the eternal questions about the meaning of the universe—so raw.

I wrote back. Of course I did. In my letter, I spoke of connection. I poured my heart out—I spoke of this new bond between us, gratitude, the gift that they gave us so selflessly. We have a beautifully strange bond.

It is hard when you have taken the path that we have, not to question why. That tiny GIGANTIC word that both the grief-stricken and the saved utter for different reasons. This endless word that played on my lips a thousand times along this journey. I have only found one answer:

Because, Love. That is why. For me, that is always why. For a thousand reasons in a thousand ways, because love.

I hope it surrounded you this year—and even if you were too blind, grieving, desperate, angry, tired, burdened, defeated, resentful, bitter, distracted, jealous, depressed, anxious, busy or all of the above, to see it. It was there. Look for it next time. Hold onto it in the darkness as you lay by your sick child. It is keeping her alive.

Reach for it. Grasp on to it. Because, Love.

# Chapter 3

# LESSONS FROM BATTLE

I've rarely grown from a comfortable place in life. This rocky path has shaped me into a better version of myself (trust me, I've got room to grow more). The things I've learned are countless, but let me try: 1) surrender can be gorgeous, 2) I don't always know what's best for me, 3) advocate—my voice is important, 4) the people who show up are the right people, 5) the people who don't show up are sparing me, 6) staying present is the best gift I can give myself in most situations, 7) the future is all imagination, 8) everything is done for us, not to us, 9) I can be better or bitter and that is my choice, and 10) it is impossible to be unhappy when you are grateful.

Well, now, you don't need to read this chapter, do you? Just kidding. This chapter's theme is that of Wabi-Sabi—have you heard of it? Another Japanese term that describes the beauty in imperfection, the patina of age, the simplicity in life, and wear, and tear. Before kintsugi, there is wabi-sabi - appreciating your patina, your wear. For me, appreciation had to come before the repair, before the filling in of my cracks with gold. I am changed, and even the kintsugi sparkling, one can still see my wabi-sabi: the gray hairs, the droopy corners of my mouth where stress took its hold permanently. They are mine. Find your wabi-sabi here.

## Hardship Is a Master Sculptor

"Wabi-Sabi" is the Japanese word for the appreciation of imperfection where age, asymmetry, and simplicity are held in the highest regard. The aesthetic is sometimes described as one of beauty that is "imperfect, impermanent, and incomplete."

Most of us spend our time fighting imperfection. We color gray hair, we wear hats to cover bald spots, we put on makeup, we use beauty creams and Botox, we get facelifts and breast implants, we take pills to grow hair and buy wax to remove it, we suck in our guts and we bleach our teeth. I am just as guilty as everyone else in my quest for a "perfect" body image and the self-criticism that comes with that unreasonable goal.

What am I saying about the gift my body has given me? All these wrinkles, these scars, these gray hairs were EARNED. We are survivors. Each imperfection is a testament to survival—to victory over hardship. If I truly embraced this, I would stop fighting the sands of time and embrace the beauty of imperfection. My hardships are master sculptors who have carved my triumphs, my strength, my power, all over my perfectly imperfect physical body. How grand we all are!

On this day, count the rings on your tree! Your triumph is gloriously etched upon you and within you.

## 20 Things My Scars Have Taught Me

I just got carded a couple of days before my 40th birthday. I fought the urge to jump the check stand and hug the woman fiercely. Apparently I don't wear the wars I've fought on my face. Lucky me. So today I stand here, weary warrior, tattered ninja, reflecting on my last decade. My 30s were a place where "self-assured woman becomes mother and fights epic battles to keep herself from drowning."

What will the 40s bring? One thing is for certain: everything I need to know was sure as heck not covered in kindergarten. A few big lessons I have learned along the way:

1. A partner who can make me laugh is worth his weight in gold. Never underestimate comic relief. Sometimes it's the only way you survive.

2. There is nothing more valuable than good health, and there is no replacement for exercise and healthy food.

3. Few things will test you more than being powerless to help your sick child.

4. It is okay for people not to like me—finding this out is a gift—now I know where my valuable time should not be spent. (see #5)

5. Adults are just scared little children on the inside—every single one of us. Everyone has wet the bed before. 99.9% of the time, what people say and do has nothing to do with you.

6. I'm wary of people trying to sell me something—whether it be a beauty product, a kitchen utensil, a cleaning product, or a religion. It usually costs more than the sticker price.

7. I become like the people I surround myself with—these days I choose carefully.

8. It really is all in my head—suffering is optional.

9. One can't fight a war without a lot of soldiers. The people who don't fight with you are sparing you.

10. The single most accurate word in the universe? Maybe.

11. When the chips are down, it will always surprise me who actually shows up. It's the best kind of surprise.

12. Don't take anything personally (see #5)—still working on this one.

13. Be your own cheerleader. Make your own Fun Cup.

14. The hardest battles I have ever fought will either break me or better me, and it really is MY CHOICE as to which one.

15. It's all about connection: relationships are what I will truly hold dear at the end of my life and it's important to remember that now.

16. The future is all imagination. If this is the case, I might as well project something great.

17. Life isn't meant to be serious. We're all just a bunch of idiots trying this messy thing out together. Laugh at myself as often as possible. Laughing at others helps too. We are all idiots.

18. No one can truly understand, except God and me. Dropping this expectation is an incredible gift to both of us.

19. Gratitude is the second most powerful force in my toolbox.

20. Forget everything you just read—I don't know anything, actually. Make your own list. After all, I once thought a sick child was the worst that could happen to me.

I earned my battle scars. I wouldn't want to change my life for anything. It's a beautiful battle. Bring on 40, world. This tattered ninja is ready for it.

"We've been planted on this rock, but we want to do more than just cling to it. We want to bloom."

*Hilary and Shiloh, paddle-boarding in Montana 2023*

## The Timer Is Running

But I have no idea how much time is on that invisible dial. How long do I have before time runs out on her little heart? How long do I have before time runs out on mine? Each moment may be our next to last with Shiloh—how can I not soak it up?

I've begun a tradition to pick a word for each new year. Last year, my word was "Fearless" and I sure was! It was a triumphant and beautiful year for all of us.

Even so, that timer is still ticking. It seems at times the pupils of my daughter's gray-green eyes turn into little clocks. I wish they had the answer: how long do I get to keep her? Instead, I choose to love reality: the only moment is now. So instead there are beautiful cheeks to kiss and chubby little handholds to absorb into my skin. I memorize her in the dark as she falls asleep in my arms. I want to be present for every moment of her life. Heck, I want to be present for every moment of MY life. I am far from there yet, but maybe, just maybe this next year...

Therefore, my word for this year is Presence. I am working on minimizing things that take me away from reality, like social media and carrying my phone with me everywhere I go. You'd think it was a golden cow the way we worship these glowing shrines in waiting rooms and post office lines. I want to connect with the snow falling outside the waiting room windows. I want to fall in love with silence. I want to make the twenty-something a little uncomfortable by striking up conversation and I want her to leave my presence with a curious smile.

And I've made a commitment to be in harmony with reality as best as I can. For me, that includes doing the Work of Byron Katie®, a woman who has revolutionized the process of enlightened thought and living. I survived a failed surgery in Boston with a smile on my face thanks to her. I've gone through two open heart surgeries without The Work® and two open heart surgeries with it, and the difference was radical.

I am also committing to meditating every day. I set my alarm at 6AM and no matter what, I sit. For 20 minutes, an hour, I connect with the divine in me. And the most surprising result? I'm not as lonely. I don't yell half as much, I soak up every moment, and my girls can see the difference in me. I feel as if my life is more rich, more colorful. And even though that timer is ticking away the hours, at least I'll have a little less regret about how I used them.

I wish for your connection to the Divine in the New Year. Whatever that means for your heart.

## Surrender to Win

Many who know me personally know that I set goals to focus on one area of my behavior that I feel needs refining. The following is my new goal: give up the need to be right.

So many times in a conversation and especially in an argument, my ego takes the baton and runs with it. If I could step outside my body during an argument, I'd see a scared woman who desperately needed to be right in order to protect her delicate self-worth and ego. Being right is the flag I'm trying to capture on the enemy's territory. Ironically, this is not a winning strategy as I emerge tattered from the battle rather than victorious.

There are few satisfactions in this life like the moment one wins an argument or, after a heated debate, it is concluded that they are right. Was the argument worth the scars of battle though? How long did the feeling of triumph last? For me, it is very briefly enjoyed, and considering how hard I fight to be right, it doesn't appear to be a sufficiently satisfying outcome.

I go back to the beginning of the argument. I see the moment that my ego wants to step in: there are two different opinions on the table suddenly, and I witness my ego gathering weapons to battle. This is where, if I want peace, I stop—I let the other person be right (even if I truly believe they are wrong). What is sacrificed? Ego and the war. Suddenly I surrender, and my soul captures the white flag of freedom, peace, truce, stillness. Rather than go to battle, we both become content and sit in each other's presence, free from resentment and conflict.

I am trying to give up the war. To die to my enemy one argument at a time. It is the humble pie that my ego needs to feast upon. I surrender; I win. Letting go always feels lighter.

*My dear friend made these for me to break. Letting them go was more powerful.*

## Take Back My Life Song

A friend made some plates for me during a period early on in our journey when my daughter had been admitted for seven straight months, and then readmitted again shortly after. She thought that by breaking them, I could release some of the anger I felt. It was a rough time. She was a good friend. It was a great idea, but I could never let go of these things I felt that defined me.

When I started writing this letter, I started listing all we've been through, the surgeries, the PICC lines, the cardiac catheterizations, countless X-rays and blood draws. The numbers were staggering. But I did something more powerful after I wrote all that.

I erased it all.

Yes, the battles we've fought have shaped us, but I don't want it to define us. I want to move forward with a stronger backbone, a resilience, a sense of accomplishment that only a soldier can feel after they've crossed the battlefield and made it to the other side.

I want to focus on our victories. I want to live in the moment. I am done being the ant under the magnifying glass of the universe.

We are not victims. We are warriors.

We are artists, musicians, writers, friends, dancers, singers, children of a powerful Creator—there is so much more to us than our pain, than our past. It's enough that the hard stuff happened once, twice, twenty times. When I relive it, it's me doing the hurting, not the past. This war where I fight both sides stops. This is our fight song. Bring back our life song. I'm taking back ownership of our present and our future, and while it may be uncertain and a little more precarious than most, it is gorgeous and it is OURS. We will bloom on this rock we are planted upon!

I'm grateful to not be fighting a big fight now—so very grateful. To those that are, this day will come. And when the dust settles, you will have a choice:

To be better, or to be bitter.

It really is that simple, but everyone's path is different, and the road I've been walking to get to this place has been bumpy. It's been a dozen-year journey so far, and while I'm still a little damaged, I'm happy. If you have questions about how I got to this place, I'd love to hear from you.

I don't need to break those plates anymore. I set them gently in the garbage and thanked God for giving me these challenges, and that particular friend at a time I needed them both.

"I whisper goodnight every night to another child's heart. I do it for a mother with empty arms."

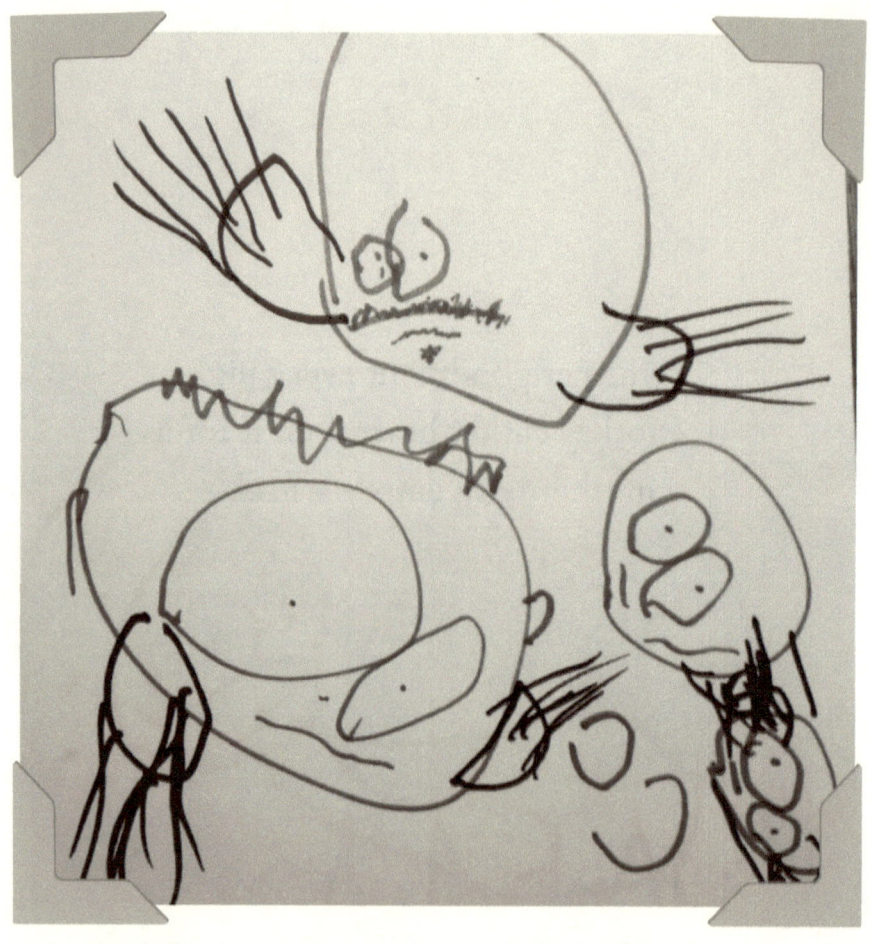

Juna's family portrait in Boston--grateful for four of us in it.

## A Change of Heart 2.0

In 2013, we spent three months waiting for Shiloh's perfect Gift of Life. I thought that the minute we received this gift that I would do cartwheels straight out of the hospital into the parking lot. We would be free! Instead, starting at 6:00 a.m. on October 11th, my 11th wedding anniversary, shock set in. We had woken up to a call that they had found a donor for Shiloh.

Once at the hospital, doctors and nurses ran to her room to congratulate us. Congratulations? Did they know that someone's child died? My mind could not leave the side of a mother deep in grief, somewhere out in the world. Shiloh went to the OR at 5:00 p.m. that evening. At 7:30 p.m., we received a call that the heart was being retrieved. I could almost hear a mother crying, hundreds, perhaps a thousand, miles away.

One in 100 babies born have a congenital heart defect—did you know that? Four years ago, I had no idea what the inside of a Cardiac ICU looked like. Now I look at four places at my dining table and am keenly aware of a family missing one seat.

Today I whisper goodnight every night to another child's heart. I do it for a mother with empty arms. This is the face of organ donation.

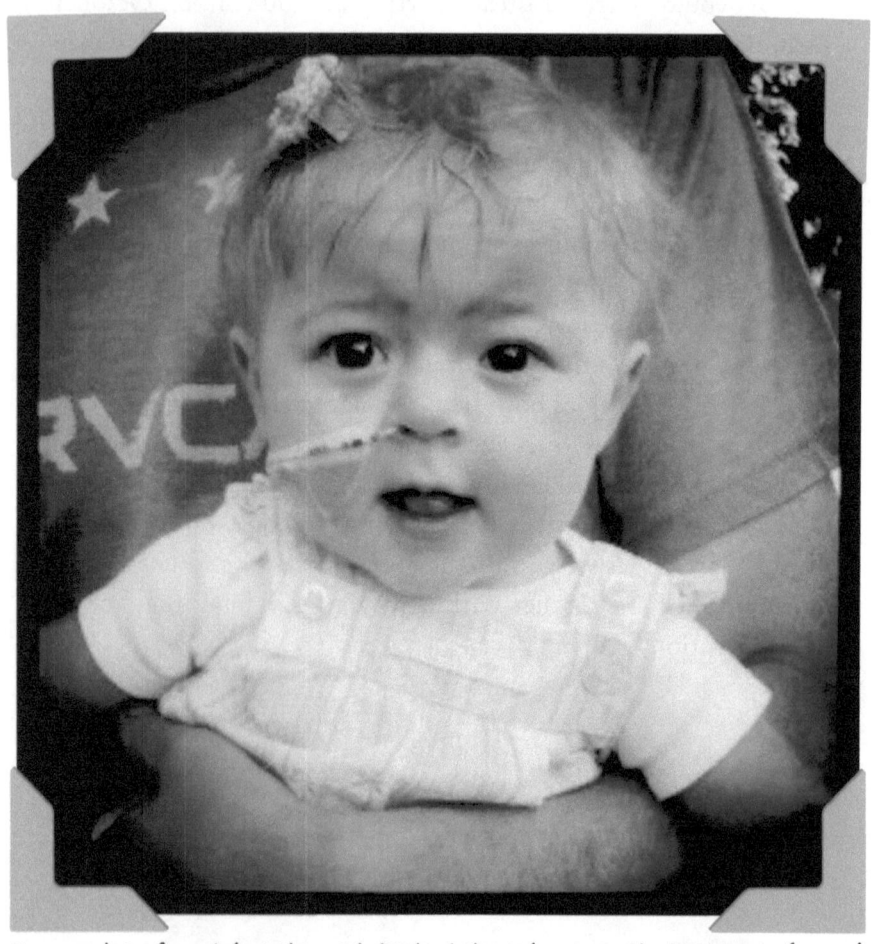

It was a lot of work but this girl ditched the tube 3 months later, 2012 (6 mos)

## This, Too, Will Make Me Stronger

On the verge of admitting my little one to the hospital to place a feeding tube. It feels like the end of the world, but it is not. She hasn't had one since she was nine months old, and it feels remarkably like the most stinging defeat three years later. I survived it then and so did she. In loving lemons, I believe that this nutrition will make her stronger and this suffering will make me stronger. It is all I can believe—the alternative is despair.

Here is an excerpt from the memoir I wrote and never published (it served its purpose—my therapy throughout our journey). Can you sense a theme? In Shiloh's name, please go out and love your lemons. Looks like I have to dust off that old file. Everything is beautiful if you look at it right.

------------

### Helping, Not Hurting (Excerpts from an Unpublished Memoir, 2014)

I'm not a doctor, but I play one in my living room.

Casually, and cooing softly, I measure the length of her nose to her earlobe and to an inch below where her sternal bone ends. I mark that with a permanent pen on the tube. Breaking open the single-use packet of lubricating jelly, I dip in one end. Taking a deep breath, I think, "This is helping my baby not hurting my baby," and I lay her down on the flowered living room rug.

Glancing to my right, I make sure I have laid out the items I need: the cushy "landing pad" for her tube and a square of clear skin-friendly tape. I steel myself, and, crawling toward her sweet sparkling eyes and wiggly baby body, I gently pin Shiloh, arms and all, between my knees. Now I need to be quick, because as she glances up at the ointment-slathered tip of that yellow tube, she suddenly knows what is about to happen.

The screaming starts.

"Helping not hurting helping not hurting" plays over and over in my head, trying to drown out the wailing of my seven-month old baby, I focus. Deep breath.

With my left hand I lift up her head, bringing her chin to her chest, closing her windpipe (briefly, to close off the opening to her lungs). Swiftly, deftly, I insert the tip of the tube into her nostril. I advance it, it hits her vagus nerve and she coughs, gags, screams a gargled, muffled cry. I push further until the black mark I have made touches her nostril. Placing the landing pad gently under the tube to prevent friction, I am nearly about to implode from the screaming, the choking. I tape, painstakingly careful to do it right the first time. Quickly, Hilary. This is easily the longest sixteen seconds of your life.

Taking the stethoscope chest piece in my left hand and holding it to her belly, I place it on her stomach. I push air into the feeding tube with a syringe. I try to hear through her crying where the sound lands. If I hear it in the tummy, I am happy. If I hear it in the lungs, I am not. Luckily, I have never had a tube land in the lung—the trick is that her chin touches her chest when I place it. A smile briefly breaks the tight rope that is my mouth as I think of the ICU nurses I love, and their handy tips for a do-it-yourself doctor.

In one motion, Shiloh is out from between my knees: I am holding her, rocking her, soothing her, soothing me. I file this experience deep inside my brain where all mommies put memories of scenes like this: putting the old family dog to sleep, placing a screaming feverish child in a cold bath, handing a baby over to an anesthesiologist. These are the tasks that feel so opposed to all things "mommy" that you have to force yourself against everything natural to complete them. Every instinct in a mom's body suffers a primal upheaval in doing so, as the brain screams "helping not hurting helping not hurting!" I'd like to picture that file sitting in a corner of my brain one day, collecting dust, unused and forgotten, helping me, not hurting me.

———————

The memoir I was writing, like most hard moments like this (in a metaphorical way), lays in a drawer collecting dust. I'm grateful I wrote it and even more grateful I don't have a need to read it. But, a dozen years later, I stand in amazement at my strength. At the fact that I've been able to rebuild her trust, that she has no memory of scenes like this.

She does not carry it—nor shall I.

## This Beautiful Rock

And it occurred to me that these hikes we took together were only a metaphor for the bigger journey. I hold her hand, I help her over the big boulders, sometimes she walks by my side when the path is smooth. I want to always be there, her scaffolding, for this rocky life. What else is this thing called motherhood? It's my duty, yes; more than that though, it's my privilege. We've been planted on this rock, but we want to do more than just cling to it.

We want to bloom.

# Chapter 4

# CAREGIVER LOVE SONGS FROM THE TIRED POET

I have a special place in my heart for special kids and their mamas. Dads, too; they play a huge part obviously (in my life, Eric is the guidewires, the traction and secure gear that lets me dangle precariously on the steepest cliffs while he shouts encouragement from below), but I *understand* the mamas. These are the love songs we should sing to ourselves as we hold these sick babies on our hips and climb those mountains. We were created for this, and it is an honor to parent these little gifts from God. It is sacred and it is hard.

I studied paleoanthropology and forensic osteology briefly in college. Did you know you can tell by the bones of the pelvis how many children a woman likely had in her lifetime? Like rings on a tree. Sometimes the cracks from motherhood aren't visible. But, yet, we get up each day and do it again, sometimes needing to catch our 923rd wind.

Hopefully this is a little more wind beneath your wings; a few nuggets of gold to melt down and fill in those cracks.

"Still, you fought this fight because no one else could. You did it all with a sick child on your hip."

## To the Tattered Ninja on Mother's Day

Hey mama with a sick child—this isn't another iron you have in the fire, darlin'—this is a breath. Sit down and take it with me. Brush aside the medical bills on the office desk. Put them out of sight. This anthem is for you—it is your fight song. Sing it with me.

This song is for you because you're tired. If you're like me, you spent the night crouching beside a pulse-ox machine wondering when you should page the doctor. You didn't sleep much. You thought about all the times you've balanced between a child at home and one in the hospital. You prepared yourself to do it again.

Fueled by love and running on fumes, you work all day and then come home to hungry small people so you work all night. You managed menus and homework and playdates and picking up toys and you ordered an oxygen concentrator and arranged a birthday party and haggled with that bloodthirsty insurance company again. You worried so much you thought it'd eat you alive. Still, you fought this fight because no one else would. You did it all with a sick child on your hip.

How can you, how can anyone question how GLORIOUS you are? Like the strongest metal, you've been proofed in the fire.

I get it, though—you're tired. You've consumed your body weight in chocolate and coffee this last week, and it still wasn't enough. But here's the thing: Late at night when the house is soothed by your hard work, when you watch little chests rise and fall so softly, this struggle doesn't matter anymore—it's behind you now. You WON. You are still upright and breathing, Mama. You are half ninja, half nurse, and 100% a prize fighter. You knocked out ONE HECK OF A YEAR. That is your gift. And only you could do it.

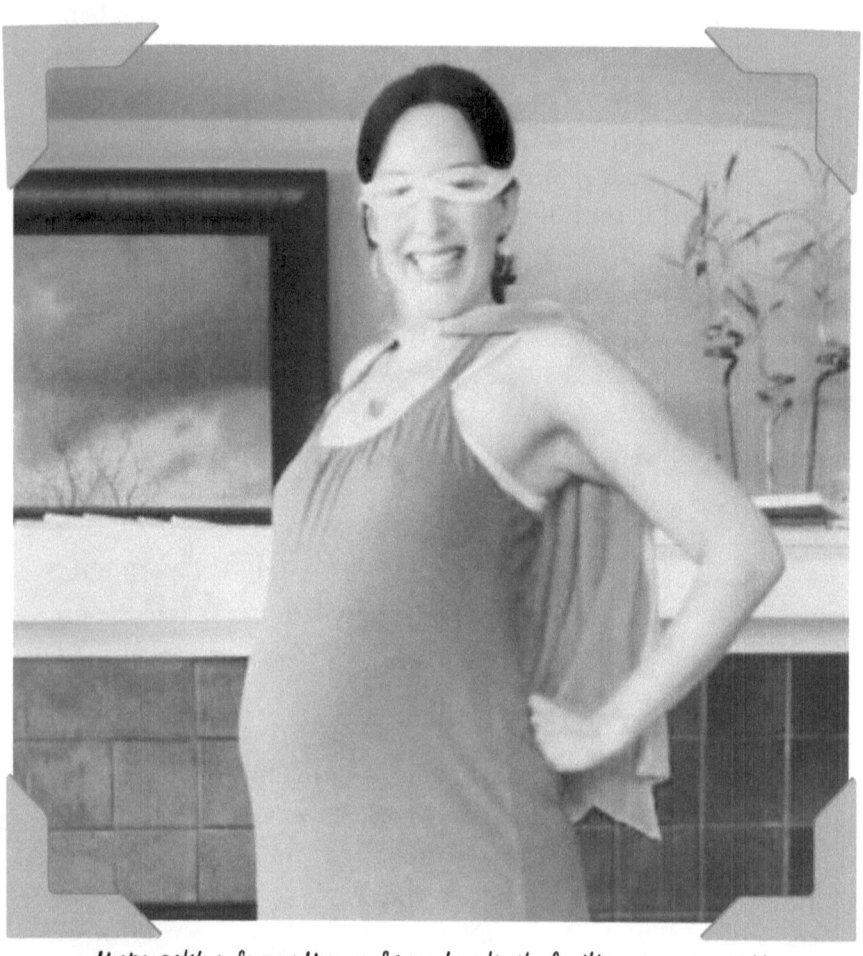

Matryoshka. Super Mama. Scared as heck. Smiling anyway. 2011

# Chiseled Mother, a Poem

I honor this body
This matryoshka

The delicate lines of my eyes
Like tissue paper
Crinkled from sun beams
Washboards slow the momentum
of tears

These ears, these conches
That entombed the beeping screaming alarms
Echoing endlessly on exhausted drives home
Mercifully quieting with age

This mouth
Which broadcasts comforts, screeches, praise
Fractures the tightrope of vexation

These beautiful, perfect arms
That embraced defeat
Carried a child to the surgeon's knife
Willing arms
That waved, furrowed, aching,
Sturdy farewells

This heart that beats out
The anthem of the womb
I Am
I Am
I Am

A womb
That is the definition of Creation

Bringing forth what does not exist
Into existence
Torn out of me
With upheaval and sanguine waves of nurture

These knees that caught me
When my frame buckled
Unable to support my grief

These marks, stretched
Yawning tiger stripes
Where my body gave room
Shimmer as silver reminders of a past shape

These feet
Planted. Supporting.
Rooted even in motion, substantial
Pacing halls, hospital rooms
Threshing carpets bare-threaded

I am the red rock slot canyon
Worn smooth, fissured, curved
Sculpted
By this flawed, coarse life

This body is a shrine
A Holy place, a pilgrimage
A masterpiece painted stroke by stroke
By the breathtakingly exquisite nourishment
Of not getting what I want.

Breathe that in,
Chiseled edifice of the Mother,
Slather it like salve into your stripes,
You silver tiger.

## Heart Mamas, a Poem

We're drafted into this battle by surprise, so we gather and the veterans brace us, embrace us.

Because it's hard.

And we fight separately but together, we celebrate the small victories, we earn the defeats, we rise and rise again

And it's hard.

We dedicate ourselves to the battle that takes everything, we fight on our knees, we celebrate on the hilltops, it's lonely. So we gather where understanding truly comes.

We know it's hard.

And when one of us falls
It aches
We lose our footing.
And it's hard
Not to feel like fish in a barrel

But we gather, we rise again, we carry our wounded, and we keep fighting. Our mission feels both heavenly and hellish and we strike that balance on the edge of a cliff before diving in. Every day. Some days it feels like too much and others it feels like not enough. Glorious days where the sun shines, memories are golden, and we forget, give us fuel. But this battle for the heart is only earthly.

Our angels feel temporary. Our miracles feel limited, yet endless. Our joy is immense because it is hard won.

We are grateful.
We are tired.
It is beautiful
It is heavy.
It is miraculous.
And it is hard.

"This body…a masterpiece painted stroke by stroke by the breathtakingly exquisite nourishment of not getting what I want."

## Forever Scars

Tattoo this moment onto my brain: dusk breaking through the blinds in an otherwise dark room. The careeek, careek, careek of the rocking chair on the hard woods, scratching forever scars. The warm lump of cherubic weight in my arms. Write with indelible ink those birds she calls eyelashes, perched on those white peach cheeks. Fold into me the tousled blond curls, dingy with play and sunscreen, falling on my shoulder. Burn, burn, burn into me the tiny hand grasping three of my fingers. The dimples in her knuckles, the whish of her breath, her small, warm butterloaf feet against my knee. Sear this moment in with needles so deep that it always seems like today, suspended in time, captive. Leave me the details.

For these moments, fleeting, raw, tender, were nearly plundered from me in times where panic screamed much louder than the gentle careek careek careek of this tired mother's rocking chair. But for now, peace.

Bring on the ink.

Let this image be burned into the undercarriage of my eyelids so that I see it when I sleep. Let my dreams be filled with this glorious cherub.

So fleeting this moment, so exquisite, this painful ink.

*Sometimes I stumble across miracles. Sisterhood. 2021.*

## Dear Sister in the Back Seat

Oh, sister. You didn't know where Mama had gone but she went far from you, and when she returned, a frazzled, somehow emptier version of her reappeared. You watched her on the phone as she fought with men you couldn't see and you heard the words "bill," "insurance coverage" and you were sure (you were almost certain) it was about you. You learned of this thing you hadn't met, called "sister" in a place called "hospital" whose name always brought a sting of pain onto Mama's face. You heard Mama cry on the inside of a shut bathroom door when she was supposed to be in the shower. You watched as this Sister took her away–again, and again, and again, for unknown things, unknown reasons, but you knew it wasn't good. You knew you had needs, too, but they had to wait.

Just yesterday it seemed, Mama had a bump on her belly but you were her world. She was your safe and happy place. Life had changed suddenly and you were left trying to catch up, to make sense of it all. This Mama who seemed so broken, didn't seem like the same one who left for the hospital a month or more ago.

You know your sister had something wrong with her heart, and you weren't certain what it was, but you felt a gaping hole in your heart, too. And when that thing that took Mama away finally came home, it had tubes trailing out of it like an alien that made strange noises and cried in your living room. What happened to your magical life with Mama?

Oh sister, I see you. Growing up next to someone who you often saw as "more special." I can tell you that your Mama tried. She woke up early before you did, drove to the hospital to meet the doctors as they rounded, to spend time with another piece of her heart, make decisions, fight for a little life, fight to keep her family of four from cracking even further apart. Stretched, being the glue holding the pieces that spanned miles, talking to you on the phone, arranging grandma visits and making sure Daddy could find your favorite blankie.

She'd rush home in the late afternoon, machines beeping in her ears while in traffic, making sure the person who had agreed to spend the evening with Sister was on their way to the hospital room where she had tearfully said "goodbye" once agaiin, trying to wipe the strain of the hospital off her face, huffing down a muffin from the hospitality cart. Never feeling like she was with the child who needed her created a hunger that food never fixed.

She'd take a big breath as she walked in the back door, praying you were still asleep in your afternoon nap. She'd quietly slip off her coat and slip in next to you in the warm covers, taking you in her arms, wanting to be the first thing you saw when you opened your eyes.

She'd play with you when you woke, and cook you dinner, and help you get on jammies and brush your teeth. She'd read you a bedtime story, all the while thinking of Sister, who was going to sleep with Mama's friend, or a nurse, or no one. Oh, how your Mama wished she could Xerox herself, night after night, day after day, so she could repair the torn feeling she felt for seven long months.

And when you fell asleep in her arms, she'd drag her weary body to the bathtub and cry softly as she washed off her day. And then she'd go to bed, and do it again. And in the morning, she'd imagine your sweet little voice saying "Where's Mama" as she drove to the hospital. Groundhog day for the Divided Mama.

You wrote a short story in 7th grade about Mama disappearing and it broke her heart a bit, but she knows that, like your sister, you have scars too. But. dear Big Sister, I hope you see the beauty in your life from the pain of childhood. That learning to love a life that isn't perfect, that contains sacrifice, and sickness, and feels fragile and a lot more weird than other families you meet—it carves you into the woman you are meant to be. Your Sister has no tubes now, but the way she looks at you, as if you hang the moon, tells me she's always been connected. And when you two fight, I pray you both find the connection in sisterhood that got a rocky start, and work to repair it. I pray you have the time to do so.

Dear Sister in the back seat, you never took a back seat, did you know that? You filled your Mama up on really hard days, and sometimes it was your healthy body that restored her perspective when the world looked sick. You are not a victim of circumstances, but a powerful child of God who was chosen to join an army of warriors. Your art comes from your struggles, and you create masterpieces from your pieces.

What I realize as the Mama Who Tried Her Best, is that your scars are yours to heal. We all have them, and those cracks that came in childhood have the potential to let a LIght into the world that is precious. Over time, I trust that you will become your own Kintsugi Master Craftsman, finding ways to fill your brokenness with gold.

I see your beauty already. You were wonderfully made, big sister. Know this.

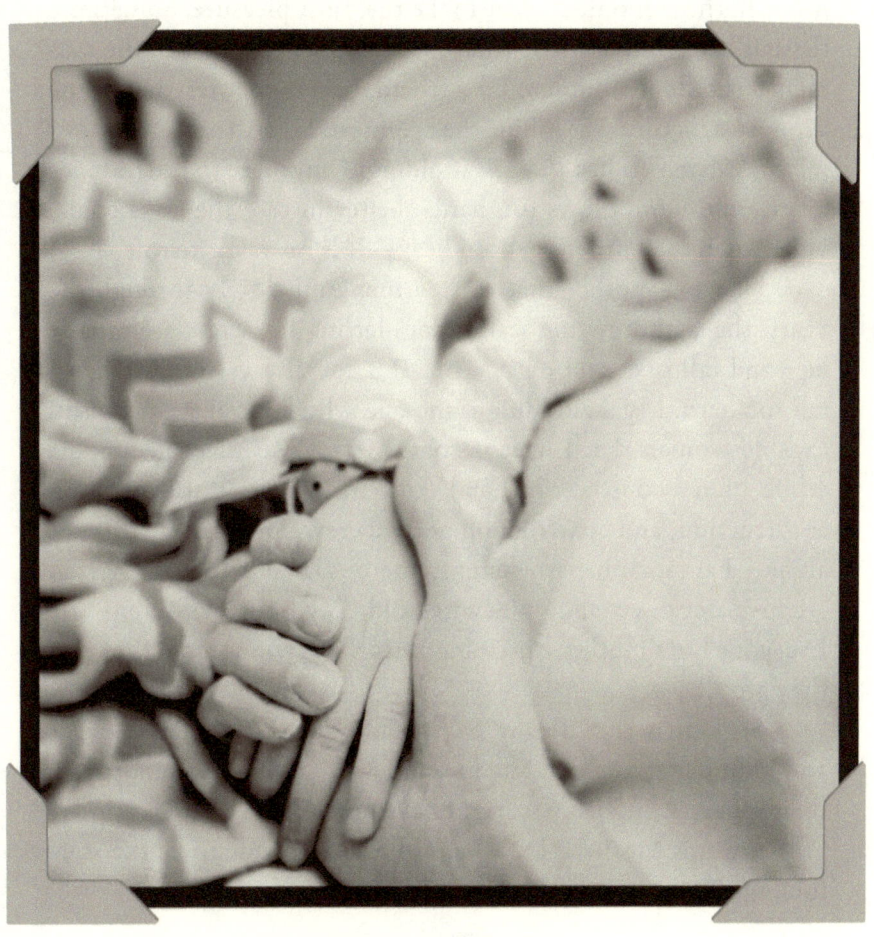

*Scaffolding. The best job.*

## Scaffolding

Sometimes I love being the one-man band. The doer, the shiner, the (let's be honest) even spotlighted. I love accomplishing and succeeding. Most of us do. I know I'm capable, strong. But it is not in those moments that I take the most pleasure. Sometimes there is better use for my strength. It is in service. It is in the moment I shoulder a burden, lift a friend, become a safety net or the support structure that I shine the brightest. I'd say that my greatest job of "Mama" is just that: Scaffolding. I am there to be the brace in case the wind blows too hard, shelter in case the rains come, yoke when the burdens get too heavy. It is my favorite role.

I have a mother that carried me. And slowly through the years, she withdrew the scaffolding, letting me wobble on shaky legs and fall over and over again. But she always comes when I fall too hard. My scaffolding is the one who created the powerful capable woman that I have become. That "Me" needed support while under construction, and trust me, there is still ongoing construction, and construction needs a crew. So my mother is not alone—I am fortunate to count numerous friends and family who are my safety nets and guidewires and they have scaffolding too. Everyone has a mother, and sometimes they are not biological, but they are all crucial.

So I sit here with my baby while she gets what she needs and I am her safety net. She knows I will catch her, support her, shelter her through any storm. I have proven myself to be sturdy.

On this Mother's Day, I am filled with pride to be the scaffolding. Construction never looked so sweet.

"Because I know that the best gifts most often come in painful, prickly packages. But oh, that infinitely priceless treasure the package contains!"

## Gifted Heart

I'm in love with this story. This glorious tale of you and me against the world. This fight of one golden heart, gifted from an angel, sewed in a patchwork of struggle and spirit. Your caged heart, fierce, beating the song of our life together.

I love this song of us, listening to you in the darkness: breath that was fought-for, hard won; golden. My arms wrapped around your sleeping body: a tender warrior. I breathe in the stillness of this hard-won peace, the war cries of the past rest, ready at our lips to do battle again. But not now.

Now, just beat, golden heart. Beat on.

This gilded cage that rises and falls on my arm houses a miracle that beats a thousand times more than was ever promised. It is a beautiful story carved into our sacred scars.

Rise, fall, golden heart. We are using up all of our stardust with this living we do. Let's burn this story into our memories, seared deeply, until the last sunset we share. But for now, sleep little warrior. We've earned this fiery sunrise.

Another gifted day, golden heart.

## Love Lemons

Last night, she lay sleeping, dreaming. I pulled up her covers and the thought arises, "Does she know?"

Does she know how close she came to not being in that bed? Does she know how many times I held her, memorizing her face, just in case it was the last time? Does she know how many times I cried, begging God for her life? Does she know what tomorrow means?

I do.

It means she has survived to walk through the doors of pre-school for the first time tomorrow. It means her mommy has survived too. Tomorrow does not even bring with it a microscopic drop of sadness. It brings triumph, on the wings of the hardest battle we have ever fought. I push back a wisp of gray hair and relish the wrinkles on this body of a warrior. I feel strongly about suffering. It's gorgeous.

I felt so strongly, I wrote a book about it.Some people change their lemons—add sugar, squeeze them until they're unrecognizable. I cherish mine, because I know that the best gifts most often come in ugly, painful, prickly packages. Like a heart defect. Unwrapping these gifts can draw blood, change the hue on beautiful brown hair, cause waves to gather around foreheads and eyes. But oh, that infinitely priceless treasure it brings!

Rich beyond all measure am I. So, this morning I, faithful protectress, ninja warrior heart mama extraordinaire, walked my delicate beauty up the stairs and said goodbye. I felt her soft, chubby little hand let go of mine. She has no idea what today was worth.

I do.

## Warriors Who Garden Well

Parents of medically-fragile children know how to read lab results; they organize their shelves and drawers with pink hospital tubs; they talk in abbreviations (CMV, WBC, EBV, IV, ICU, O2 the list goes on and on and on); they always have an overnight bag in their car when they go to the doctor; they have a lot of home medical equipment that they've rented so long they now own; their kids play in sprinklers with IVs and PICC lines which they are pro's at flushing (they can do a mean hep-lock); they troll for extra medical supplies on the way out of the hospital; they have a list of nurses (naughty and nice) that is registered with the hospital; they've made friends with the nice nurses; they hug longer, cherish small milestones like riding in a car seat (they celebrate a lot more than your average Joe); their wrinkles are as much from smiling as stress.

Their "normal" is not your "normal." Their capacity is not more, it's just different. The only time you should feel sorry for a parent of a complex kiddo is when they lose their child, because, trust me here, the ones with living children know. They are doing the happy dance (they might be too tired to move but it's there if you look hard enough) because their child is ALIVE, and like a garden well-tended, the fruits of their hard labor is oh, so plentiful.

We are warriors, scarred from the battlefield and still kneeling, tending our gardens. I cannot see that it gets better than that.

We are the lucky ones.

# Chapter 5

# SHIFT HAPPENS: PERSPECTIVE IS EVERYTHING

Trauma can change our brains. We start out as "glass half-full people" and then trauma happens, hurt happens, sickness and death happen, and suddenly we notice the air in the glass. It's human. But the glass hasn't changed—it's our perspective that has changed. And the problem is that a negative perspective doesn't serve us—it actually makes the situation harder to endure. Study after study shows that more positive people are more resilient people. And more resilient people are more successful at accomplishing what they set out to do, simply because when they encounter roadblocks or hardships, their attitude helps them navigate a way around or through them. They just don't give up as easily, and they also tend to enjoy life more. I learned that the hard work I put in shifting the way I saw my world, the better my world looked, and the easier my path became. I'm blessed to help people see this every day in my practice, and it changes lives. This isn't Polyanna - this is being conscious of where I put my energy. Every situation has a Light and a Dark to it. Where I choose to focus is everything. If trauma, betrayal, and disappointment has you focusing on the darkness more than you used to, I'm here with your lantern.

"If you truly love who you are, if you truly love your child, how could you wish to change anything that brought you both to this place?"

## Look Down

The last day of the year is an excellent time for reflection. Many had a great year. There are many others who tell the last year not to let the door hit them the butt on the way out. They bid good riddance to difficulty and look toward the new year as a blank canvas; a fresh start.

But I ask you, on the last day of the calendar year, who would you be without your difficulties? What strength would you know you had inside of you? How can you appreciate the "easy" times, the "lucky" times, the calm and peace without contrast? I see each hardship I go through as a badge of honor: a testament to my mind, body, and spirit conquering another mountain. I accessed a fight I didn't know was in me, and I made it through. Perhaps I was slightly worse for the wear, but I stand, battered, at the top of the mountain, triumphant.

We've all heard the saying, "Don't look down." I say, "Look down!" How can you steel yourself for the climb ahead of you if you don't acknowledge how far you've already climbed? Each slip of the foot teaches an invaluable lesson. Every time you lost your footing, you learned about which footholds were unsteady. You learned to trust your innate sense of balance, the guidewires that supported you on life's cliffs. And of course, the safety nets when you fell. Most importantly, you learned to get back up again.

I found a business-sized card while cleaning out my office yesterday. It said "I'm not intoxicated - I have Wilson Disease." In 2002, I was dying from the rare liver and brain disease with which I was born. I had lost my balance and wove when I walked, steadying myself on furniture and walls like a newly mobile toddler. My mouth refused to alliterate words, so I slurred like someone who had consumed a fifth of whiskey on an empty stomach. My hands failed me as well—I could no longer type. I had to leave my job at the brokerage. My husband washed my hair, brushed my teeth, and cut up my food.

My neurologist told me that I was in danger of being arrested for public intoxication and suggested I carry this card on me at all times. I began the incredibly frustrating task of learning to walk and speak again. Eventually I healed, to the bewilderment of doctors who thought I was a lost cause and let me know it was time to say my goodbyes. Grit is a thing.

And I could easily fall victim to "why me?" Twenty years later I see that my experience brought an understanding to Shiloh's journey that nothing else could. I understand being a sick kid. I understand when our bodies betray us. I have walked the walk of finding beauty in hardship. I have said my goodbyes. I have fought anyway. God said, "Shiloh, I have the perfect Mama for you." What a gift! Everyone comes to the table with the gifts they need, and everyone is taught the lessons they need to be taught. Find the good in them is my job.

Like everyone, then, I have climbed mountains big and small. Being humbled so completely when I was so ill was one of my Mount Kilimanjaros of mountains. After all, I once carried a card that defined me, excused me, in my pocket, yet here I sit, typing, walking, talking (clearly, most days...ah, coffee I thank thee). I climb now, with a kiddo on my hip.

A conqueror. Mothering another conqueror.

Look down. You have come a long way, baby. Thank you to this last year and all the years that came before. I see the value and the victory in every mountain you brought to us.

## What Is the Gift in This?

There is the most beautiful pink flower found inside of nodding thistle. I mean, please google it. Fuschia pink, unfolding so mysteriously. Yet, if you've ever walked into it on a hike, you know the pain.

The most amazing gifts come in prickly packages. What I thought was the worst thing that could ever happen to us (a sick child) has become my biggest treasure. Being a heart mom isn't always easy, but there is so much gratitude for the journey and the miracle we get to witness every day.

> The triumph.
> The life.
> Each smile.
> The beating heart.
> The breath in our lungs.
> The ability to rise again and again.
> It is all a gift.

Even in your darkest moments there have been these unexpected gifts. They come at dawn, after the storm. Some come out of the woodwork others make themselves known subtly and quietly. They even carry you through it without you even realizing it until it's over.

Can you see them?

I thought having a sick child would be the worst thing that could happen to us. Boy, wasn't that silly of me.

"I choose to have faith that
everything that has ever happened
to me has been for my greater good.
So I open my heart to find beauty
in hardship, trusting that it is there
under the pain. I trust it will reveal
itself eventually. It is worth
the search."

## A Kind Universe

Most of us carry baggage of past hurts, abuses, painful experiences. Some of us build our lives around pain, shut out everyone, building an emotional moat around ourselves and filling it with hungry crocodiles. It is easy for me to see the universe as a very cruel and hostile place. Many of you who know me and the life I have had can see where I could have made that moat. But again, we see that perspective changes everything. How we see life is a matter of choice.

Eleven years ago, Eric and I went on our honeymoon. I was finally feeling up to it after years of lying in bed very ill. We picked a Caribbean cruise and were gone about eight days. We came home to a front door slightly open, and I dropped to my knees in despair when I looked inside. Gone. Everything in our tiny little first home had been turned upside down and anything of value was gone. I felt violated, angry, and very vulnerable.

I was contacted by the police when they found the guy who robbed us. At the time when asked what I wanted done with him, I said "jail time and rehabilitation" (he was a meth addict). Had I known what a gift that robbery would be in our lives, I would have simply said, "Please thank him for us." I was still learning.

The gift revealed itself: When we decided not to replace most of the tens of thousands in stolen items, we suddenly had a nest egg. And Eric had the opportunity he was looking for to become a full-time professional artist. He has supported us by painting ever since. His twenty-five year career, marked by lots of success and accomplishments, was owed to a guy with a meth addiction who had stumbled upon our house once upon a time.

It is a conscious choice to become the alchemist and convert hostility to kindness. These gifts may not be readily understood at the time of injury. However, I choose to have faith that everything that has ever happened to me has been for my greater good. So I choose to open my heart to beauty in hardship, trusting that it is there under the pain. I trust it will reveal itself eventually. Like a friend looking for something to pawn.

If you are going through painful times, please take a leap of faith and be the alchemist that your heart needs. Can you find good in the difficulties that have happened?

It is worth the search.

## The Simple Things

There are moms, probably many of them out there in the world, whose hearts do not leap just seeing their little ones on swings. There are moms who do not remark to themselves how close they were to their five-year-old not having a hand to hold on the slide. There are moms who don't appreciate putting their child into a grocery cart or carrying their sleeping child inside after a day of playing hard on the playground. There are moms who never think about the fact that they could be decorating a grave instead of sugar cookies. There are moms who don't notice pink lips or the ability of a three-year-old to run without getting tired so fast. There are those moms who don't appreciate a cordless toddler. Some moms don't appreciate the singing of "Let It Go" in the back seat, 462 times with each one being a different version. Some moms take four places at the table for granted.

I am not one of those moms.

Sometimes life is beautifully, deliciously, gloriously...normal. Nothing but Gratitude fills my heart. The future is too bright to dwell on the past.

4th of July 2013, finally home after 3 months in Boston, 3rd surgery failing

## Oh Say Can You See

In 2013 we took the gamble of our lives, for Shiloh's life. We raised $20,000 and moved our family cross-country for an unknown amount of time, in order for her to have a rare surgery to turn her heart back into a four-chambered heart. It was huge, and it was risky, and at first it went really well, and then it failed miserably. Upon return to the high elevation in Utah, we were admitted again and again to the ICU, for different infections mainly, but in the end what was happening was heart failure.

I tried for ten days to get insurance to approve a flight back to Boston but she was too unstable, and they repeatedly denied it. It was a hard season. But it lead to some great reflection, and this is what I wrote:

Here's the Great Reveal about Shiloh's heart condition: we did not go to Boston Children's Hospital to make Shiloh's heart happy. Shiloh's heart has been and will always be happy. Her heart is not "broken." No. It is perfect!

It is *me* that is broken when I look at her and want something different than what is. Shiloh would have been happy if I had taken her home and done nothing for her perfect little heart. So please, don't ever be "sorry." We chose this life when we decided to fight for her, and we never expected it to be easy. We just get tired sometimes.

Basically we are still learning to discipline our tantrum-throwing little minds that are not getting what they want. Most days now, I get a glimpse of the truth: life is perfect. The ICU is as beautiful as my front porch and Shiloh's Heart is Happy. Shiloh and her heart have given us the gift of vision.

My eyes are still blurry, but there are those wonderful moments where the world is clear and oh so beautiful.

## Mark Your Calendars

I've had 12 years to think about this, and it has become very important to me the things I choose to let play out in this brain of mine. I have people sit on my couch and work through all kinds of trauma. What I notice is the pain they feel from reliving painful events. Some can't help it of course, and many times, though, there is a conscious choice.

If I was in a back alley in downtown Salt Lake City, and someone came around the corner, stabbed me with a knife, took my purse, and ran, that would be traumatic. And it would be really hard in that moment. That person was my perpetrator, and what he did was wrong. There is no doubt.

I wondered, though: when I relive the event, weeks, months, years later, who is my perpetrator now? The man in the alley is gone. Is he still hurting me? Or is it my brain that has taken over that work?

When I realized this, I decided to do myself a favor: remove the marks on my yearly calendar that commemorate negative events. They hurt me enough at the time—why would I do that to myself again? I could set up my day to be horrible because 'three years ago on this day' my five-pound newborn underwent a seven-hour open-heart surgery. No! It was hard enough at the time—should I further the abuse to my soul by reliving it over and over again? My year would be consumed by painful memories if I wrote them all on my calendar!

An abuse generally happens to me once, or at least for a limited season—whether it is a health crisis, a death, an abusive person in my life, an accident, or anything that does damage to my soul. I survive it the best I can, and then it is in the past. But once I start reliving it, I take over the role of abuser, inflicting suffering on myself. There is no power, no change, no action that can come from being a perpetual victim. Trust me, I've taken a ride in the victim's seat, and it got me nowhere but lost.

I am kinder to myself by letting negative events stay in the past until I choose to revisit them. I suggest to the clients in my practice that I only visit the pasI to heal or to learn. To mine them for the treasures they have given me: the lessons, the gifts, some of which can only be seen in hindsight. I learn, I process, I grow as a human. I smile more. I dwell in misery less. I learn who shows up, who I can trust, who has shown me that I can't. My calendar is freed up to celebrate great occasions, triumphs, and joy.

Who is hurting you now? And now? It is in your power to choose kindness.

"Most days now, I get a glimpse of the truth: life is perfect. The ICU is as beautiful as my front porch. My eyes are still blurry, but there are those wonderful moments where the world is clear and oh so beautiful."

## Hitting the Links

I'm offering you a change of perspective with regard to the challenges you are facing or have faced in your life. What if a divine source measured your potential and saw that you were so magnificent, so amazing, so wondrous and awesome that they had to give you a "handicap?" Much like the negative scores given to golfers, these challenges seek to make the playing field even.

I had a running joke with another special needs mama - every time something bad would happen, we'd say something like "wow! I guess we've got to keep the playing field even for the other humans, eh? Taking you down a notch to keep it fair!" It was funny...to us because we had a twisted sense of humor.

But seriously, though. From this perspective, the bigger the hardship, the bigger the potential of you, wondrous spiritual being! You must be so powerful that God has to work to keep things even! The Universe, Source, God, the Divine—whatever name you give it—is the Ultimate Score Keeper.

How did you play today?

## Intention Is Everything

I took a stance once on a very heated topic my parenting groups were discussing. My experience raising a fragile child weighed heavily in the "side" I chose on the issue. It felt like the right hill to plant my flag and die on. I was absolutely convinced.

I remember exactly where I was sitting when I read another parent's take on the issue. Here's what she said: "It's a tough issue because both sides feel like they are protecting their children."

*POP!!* I could almost feel my anger bubble deflate right then. Wow. Yes, even though I may feel that those on the other side are misinformed, they are still making their best effort in the protection of their tiny little charges.

Just like me. Woah.

Instantly, just in the process of SEEKING to understand, I had instant compassion for those parents that I was just offering (last week) a vacation to a remote and disease-ridden island. Isn't it amazing how just one sentence can alter your course through animosity and anger and take a wild U-turn towards compassion and understanding?

We are all in this together. And we will never completely understand or necessarily agree with each other. How can we? We don't have the same personalities, the same parents, the same cultures, the same spiritual beliefs, the same situations, the same children, the same 24/7/365 experience of living each others' lives. Even siamese twins see things differently. I dropped the idea long ago that "they should understand me." It's impossible. And futile. And it's just not true. And I don't need it anymore.

But, oh, when people try...the effort is everything.

# Chapter 6

# I GOTTA HAVE FAITH-A, FAITH-A, FAITH

I am a child of the '80s, and it turns out the things I sang while bopping in my legwarmers and neon were prophetic. An incredible book I read often says that we know that in all things God works for the good of those who love him, who have been called according to his purpose. I've been called to this sacred duty. And if everything is done for my good, then it becomes my job to find that. To trust that. And it can be incredibly hard. One doesn't have to believe in God to become better through trials.

This journey has built my faith more than anything could have (my faith journey was not a burning bush, but a very slow, winding and bumpy road with layovers in Buddhism, Taoism, and every organized religion from Judaism to Methodist to Evangelical and back again). I've built faith. And still I've fought and pleaded for things to be different at times. I've been frustrated and confused and downright shocked by what God puts on my plate sometimes. I believe He can handle those feelings—I can't surprise God. But I can learn—oh man, sometimes it takes me 23 lessons, but I can learn.

I've learned that I'm not broken. That Shiloh isn't broken. That what was created was perfect. That, for me, God was the original kintsugi artist—he fills my cracks with gold. He did so with Job, with Matthew, with Byron Katie, with women I've witnessed who lose their children and go on to inspire others . If I trust that all things are for my good, then things like acceptance, and purpose, and trust, and faith become a lot easier. Seeing things this way also brings peace, joy, and gratitude, which is simply more effective.

## Sacred

I've heard it said before that if we were to write our challenges and tribulations on a piece of paper, crumple it up, and throw it into the center of a room of people, and then we were allowed to pick any one of a hundred trials on the floor to take up instead, we'd most likely look for our own in that wreckage and keep them. Why? Because they are familiar. They may be weary and worn, but they are ours. Why is that? I truly believe it's because I was chosen for them. They fit me.

We are all given different crosses to bear - some physical, some spiritual, but no one escapes this earth without challenge. I've been asked if I would wave a wand and have all our challenges disappear so that my child wouldn't suffer. While sometimes this journey has been unbearable, I would not soil this sacred gift, this consecrated, holy journey, by sending it back to the Giver.

I will hold it precious, even in battle, because it is ours. Consecration is where heaven meets earth. These sacrifices, tithing. These scars, testaments.

I once read that life is 95% loss. We lose our dream, our job, our hair, our waistline, that house we wanted, that idea of a healthy child, that friendship, that scholarship, that investment, that paycheck, that parent, that dog. Loss, after loss, after loss.

I have lost a lot. We all have. But what I keep coming back to is the sacredness of the space those things leave. Grief is a beautiful dedication to something I held sacred.

Consecration is where heaven meets earth, and it is there that I see my daughter. She is holy, and so is this journey and all who share it with us. And when she is gone, I don't want to stop seeing her as sacred, perfect, consecrated. I will see her light in the places where heaven meets the earth.

Matthew, a follower of Jesus said, "you are the light of the world. A town built on a hill cannot be hidden. Neither do people light a lamp and put it under a bowl. Instead they put it on its stand, and it gives light to everyone in the house. In the same way, let your light shine before others, that they may see your good deeds and glorify your Father in heaven."

Put it under a bushel, no. I'm gonna let it shine. Let it shine, let it shine, let it shine.

"We have a greater strength that is more empowering and long-lasting: We understand ourselves, we care for ourselves, we heal ourselves, we give ourselves exactly what we need because we know that best; if we need more, we ask for what we need from the right people, and we look to God."

## The Impossible Mile

"They should walk a mile in my shoes."

Oh the pain of not feeling understood. "They don't get it." "They don't know what it's like." "They should know I'm struggling." "I need them to understand." "My husband doesn't understand." "My mother doesn't 'get' me." Ouch.

Is it true? Can anyone truly understand you? Let's look at it.

Take two people trying to understand each other. Bob and Jill. Different childhoods, different parents, different personalities, different genders. Neither of them has spent the same 365 days a week, 24 hours a day together. Even if they were Siamese twins, they have different brains. They'd experience the world about eight inches differently from each other, right?

My daughter says, "Mom, they don't *get* me." She sees her friends that don't have the scars she does, the frequent doctors' visits and lab draws, the consciousness of germs and handwashing—all the things that make her different. I tell her gently that it's impossible. They haven't BEEN you. How can they *get* you?

How can we possibly expect another human to truly UNDERSTAND?

A dozen years ago during my daughter's second open-heart surgery, my husband and I were in the waiting room. It was an eight-hour surgery, so we spent a long time in that big room full of chairs and worried parents coming and going. One particular couple seemed to be a wreck. The father pacing, the mother glancing at the door every five minutes. After a while, a surgeon in scrubs came through the door and crossed the room to them. It was a large echoey room and I overheard what he said:

"We got the tubes in her ears, Ma'am, and everything went well. She's in recovery and you can see her soon." Palpable relief. The couple hugged.

Wow. While my baby's tiny heart was being dissected and re-routed and re-sown, this little girl of theirs was getting tubes in her ears.

The comparison is painful and stark, and leaves a bitter taste in our mouth. Don't they know what we are going through? How BAD it can get? Don't they *appreciate* how mild, how small of a thing that is?

We only know what we know. I'm involved with thousands of parents of special needs kids, and thousands of parents of typical kids. Everyone has challenges that become too much for them at times. It has been a journey of awareness—and perspective for me.

It took time for me to realize, but for that couple in the waiting room, that was their biggest thing. It was their child. It was equal to an open-heart surgery. Not less than. Equal. There is no comparing. There is no spectrum of more or less or harder and easier. I can't understand what their experience was, and they can't understand mine.

Our two perspectives are too different. And that is true for every other human on this planet. I can possibly expect another heart mom to come closer to understanding, but to expect them to truly understand is impossible. They do not even experience the same procedure, the same situation in the same way. Different parents, different personalities, different perspectives.

So does that mean we're alone? No. We can drop the NEED to be understood. It's futile. Is it truly needed? Is it ever enough? Does it take the pain away? But we have a greater strength that is more empowering and long-lasting: We understand ourselves, we care for ourselves, we heal ourselves, we give ourselves exactly what we need because we know that best, we ask for what we need from the right people, and we look to God. Because that's the only being that truly knows—knows every minute of your life, every hair on your head.

It's God you look up to in the hospital room as you rock your sick baby, or stand on the side of the road with a flat tire, or get that letter in the mail with the test results, and say "Are you seeing this?? This sucks! Did you hear what they said? Be with me. Understand me. I need you."

"You *get* me."

## Trust the Sculptor

The Venus de Milo did not get created by a soft cloth. No, the sculptor's chisel was sharp and the hammer swift. Chunk after chunk of marble fell at the feet of the artist, and he did not stop until a beautiful effigy emerged from the stone.

I know how she felt. I've been carved by windstorms, hammered by the chisel of horrible news, I've faced the sandblaster over and over again in my short time on this Earth.

I like the results of my carving. And, add 20 more years of painful surrender and chipping away, and I have a feeling I'll like it even more. I am excited to see the results—I trust the process; I trust the Great Sculptor. They, in their infinite wisdom, know what they're doing. It's a Great Master, this spirit, no matter what earthly name you give it.

So today I walked through the doors of the hospital knowing that the sculptor might have a giant chisel labeled "liver cancer" on it, and I surrendered to the possibilities of that process. I breathed, I smiled through my bi-annual ultrasound. I pictured with love, the carving out of tumors through surgery, the radiation, the listing for new parts—even though I really do think that our household has reached its maximum number of transplants—I mean, c'mon. It might all be part of my destiny eventually, and I trust that it will all be for my greater good.

Today is not my day. I smile to think there are other plans in the works. Take a rest, my sculptor. More work another day.

I've learned the definition of bas-relief. Pun intended? Well, we have to have a sense of humor, even about liver cancer, or all is lost. God has one—I mean, look at the elephant seal. (I forgive you if you put down my book to google. Come back.)

"The surrendering, constant surrendering to the next decision, her next need, the new plan. Looking back on that woman who held her baby in the hospital room, silently crying, I see the miracle in that kind of love."

## Silver Linings and Open Eyes

"We just need more faith." "Wait for the miracle." "We just have to pray harder." "The Lord will heal her!"

Ooh the unintended weight of these beliefs. Desperate for a miracle for our daughter, we heard it often, we thought it often. Where was God in this? We knew what we needed, what she needed. We prayed, we begged, we prayed some more, we begged sometimes on our knees, weeping for our sick child and her future. We were told we needed a blessing to get her out of the hospital—at that point, I was ready for *every* blessing, "Come Jews, come Muslims, come Christians, come Buddhists, lay your hands on my daughter, we need a miracle." The exhaustion of begging, the fear we would not get our miracle. The constant thought of losing what we loved.

Was our faith weak? Was God deaf? What kind of God lets children suffer and die?"

Big questions about such a little soul who hung in the balance between this world and the next. Over the last 12 years, I've thought a lot about these questions. And likely I'll feel different about them in the next 12.

I see that in those moments, I wanted MY miracle. I knew what was best, I needed my child to live, to be whole, to come home with us. What I failed sometimes to see in those moments of desperate frustration was HIS miracles. The people who showed up. The people who didn't (and spared us). The surrendering, constant surrendering to the next decision, her next need, the new plan. Looking back on that woman who held her baby in the hospital room, silently crying, I see the miracle in that kind of love. I see myself upright and breathing through a tornado, through a war. I see the life in her eyes, and her closeness to Jesus, at times, reaching out to touch Him, she was so close.

What was God giving her in all of this? What was the gift in all this pain? What was He giving me? At the time, my vision was clouded with emotion, with grief. The answer to this question has revealed itself slowly over the years. When I decide to open my eyes...I find it. I notice that often in life, HIS plan was much better than MY plan.

I see miracles in the machines that kept her alive, and I see miracles when suffering ends. I see miracles in failed surgeries, and machines keeping other babies alive, and the relief parents feel when they finally make a hard decision, and I see the grace in letting go. I see miracles in grief, and honor in tears. I see a child who has had to fight for life, who sings every numbered day on this Earth, and I see God in all of it. I see things happening in HIS time, not MY time.

It is a fallen world, yes. Children are sick, children die. I recently heard another parent, suffering, say "What God lets that happen?" I understand that question. For me, it is a God who gives us the gift to experience humanity, and it is joyous, we hold new babies, we skip on the playground, feel victories, pet puppies, we finally find our car keys, we taste wonderful food and hug old friends. And it is hard, and we feel pain, heartache, loss, defeat, and it shapes us, sometimes roughly, but if we look to Him for strength, and open our eyes, we see the miracles He gives us. Death and suffering is reality. It is human. Personally, I wouldn't want to experience all of this without *that* God. I see the miracle in choosing to be better, not bitter. The courage in faith. I see a miracle in my morning coffee, another sunrise, my friend on the other end of the phone, learning to be present for my loved ones, because tomorrow isn't promised. Looking for strength when MY idea of what's best doesn't happen. I see miracles in acceptance of His will for my daughter, no matter what.

Finding that silver lining, that's where God is in your storm. Gently open your eyes to it. Look up. It's not going to be perfect—I'm still figuring it out. It's all grace. I hope you find it.

## Who Were You Created to Be?

Everyone can agree that a one-year old is a pure, innocent being. Life hasn't happened yet. They are wholesome, wondrous beings. Perfect. Innocent. Centered. Joy.

Then, life happens. Trauma. Wins. Defeat. Highs. Peer pressure. Addictions. Lows. Abuse. Betrayal. Disappointment. Lay-offs. Divorce. Victories. Losses. Surrender. Embarrassment. Imposter syndrome. Bullies. Love. Kids. Relationships of every kind. Hurt. Choices. Regret.

And suddenly we are far from our true center. Sometimes we are filled with uncertainty, fear, distrust, anger, resentment, bitterness, anxiety, low self-worth, depression, regret, grief. It hurts because IT IS NOT WHO WE ARE.

I'm grateful to have discovered a process that brings me to Center every time I use it. I'm kinder, happier, more compassionate, positive, joyous, loving, curious, creative, capable. I use it in my practice, and in my personal life, but only when I don't want to suffer.

I'm really excited about the syllabus I've created to teach these techniques, concepts and skills to other people. So far I've taught corporate leaders, teens, parents of special needs kids, young adults, and other therapeutic professionals. It has been a gift and it fills my bucket. Ironically, bringing me to my True Center.

Where and when do you feel your True Center? Do you think it's possible to stray too far away from it? How do you make your way back? Do you feel centered when you believe things like "she is suffering," "I can't do this," "they should've shown up," "he betrayed me," "she shouldn't have died?" If not, then something about that thought isn't true.

Who were you created to be?

So grateful for everything it took to have this moment. Spring 2013 before Boston..

## Do You Like Who You Are? Truly?

If so, why would you not appreciate every moment, every experience that made you who you were? If you changed one thing, took out one person, one big event or decision, would you be the same person? The same parent?

Abusive dad.

Bad boss.

Horrible ex-wife.

Special needs kiddo.

Trauma.

Faith crisis.

Grief, loss, and surrender.

Failure.

If you changed anything, any fire that sharpened your blade, you'd be a different person. And if you change the way you see things, you change your past.

The great thing about surviving something is building confidence. You know you'll make it because you have. All it requires is bravery, endurance, and a little patience.

"And this too shall pass." 2 Corinthians 4:17-18

And odds are, it'll create even something greater in you. Hang on, the miracle is coming.

## Christmas 2017: Take Shelter

Mama, I know you've had a crisis of faith. Probably several. When the world has you on your knees, it's hard to question if you can believe in anything at all, let alone an invisible being that might have put you there.

But odds are, whether you believe or not, you've heard of a young wandering couple seeking shelter in Bethlehem one night. Lost, probably scared—all they needed was a place to lay their heads. But yet there was no room in the inn.

You've been lost, vulnerable, and scared, haven't you? How many have given you shelter?

Mary found the manger she needed, and the rest that transpired changed the world. Is that child you hold tonight not just as sacred as Jesus to you? Your babe may be swaddled with hospital blankets and tubes, your holiday music may be alarming machines, but Mama, if she's breathing, miracles abound.

Hold that Holy.

The holidays can be tumultuous, stressful, grief-filled, joyous, busy, chaotic, exciting, lonesome—they can fill your heart with gratitude, and break you like a prisoner of war.

Find shelter, Mama—whether it be in a friend, a song, a prayer, a cup of tea, a book, or a hot bath. Shine that star upon your blessings, magnify them, name them out loud. You are a little someone's savior. Hear that—take it in.

Life is big—and gorgeous. Let those tears bless you. You've wandered so far, so long, so lost. It's time to take shelter.

Merry Christmas, my fellow soldiers. Merry everything.

3 years old and fearless. Yellowstone family cabin, 2014

"So keep on, keep pressing, brave girl. Together we are writing the most beautiful story."

## Fear vs. Faith

This last fall, I was overcome with fear. It was the cause behind the unraveling of my life. I was terrified of sending my oldest daughter to kindergarten (i.e., a wiggly petri dish) possibly bringing life-threatening germs home to my immunosuppressed toddler with the heart transplant. I was overwhelmed by the constant demands of a new school to come to all the events held, volunteer hours needed. I was feeling so much less than the positive Hilary I had become.

My editor wanted me to start seeking representation for my finished manuscript and I stalled, paralyzed in fear. I felt like a hypocrite, advocating positive thinking in my book and feeling dreadfully negative in real life. The thought of such a personal journey out there in the world seemed terrifyingly similar to running naked in Times Square. Vulnerable.

Once I spent three weeks in the hospital very sick. How I got there was a long boring story, but what I learned from it is important: life is short, fleeting. We do not come here to waste our opportunities by succumbing to all of our human fears. I don't know about you, but I came here to rise above fear and look toward love for my future. I have faith that all will be just as it should be. How can it be anything else?

We elected for Shiloh to get a transplant in order for her to LIVE. So we brave Sunday school and the children's museum and we revel in the fact that she's actually alive to enjoy these things. Much like her, I've gotten several new chances at life. Manuscripts currently being sent out, giving my delicate heart little wings to fly and land in someone's capable hands. The future is wild and untamable. This moment on Earth is your chance to live it, embrace it, dare it, risk it all. What else is life for? The sky isn't even the limit.

And also, sometimes limits are important. Ask anyone who's invited me to Angel's Landing (okay, I'll wait while you google again). I've learned a lot asking the question: "In choosing between faith and fear, is there a middle ground? Is it called wisdom?" I'm pretty certain that the vertigo I get when scaling heights, wouldn't be really great at the top of Angel's Landing. Sometimes fear keeps us from being reckless.

My word that year that Juna started Kindergarten was Fearless. I had been letting fear dictate my life after Shiloh's transplant. Nowadays, I tend to look for a middle ground and listen to the Spirit to find Wisdom.

What is the Spirit saying to you?

## Brave Girl

How many times have you had to be brave, little one!? How many times have I?

I know you don't always want to be. But you need to hold on. Because I believe in your future. It's bright, it's limitless. It's gorgeous.

But even more beautiful than that is NOW. Now is the chance to test your mettle. To defy the odds. To triumph in the face of adversity. God gave you this great gift. Few get a lifetime like this, angel: This second chance at breath, a rebirth—a living, breathing miracle, literally stitched into your heart?

This. God made you for this.

And in His mercy, His grace, He gave us each other. He made us fierce. Your bravery multiplies mine. We are a force to be reckoned with.

So keep on, keep pressing, brave girl. Together we are writing the most beautiful story.

In gratitude for the fight.

## Surrender

Last week, I left my severed limb in another state. Well, actually, I left my girls and got on a plane— isn't it the same thing? I didn't know if I could do it—wiping tears from my cheeks, walking through the airport, I felt lost. How could ANYONE take care of them like I do? There are so many details, so many medications, so many scheduling issues. Even the most careful caretaker like my mother was, would certainly fall short. What if something HAPPENED??

And we all know what happens in my life when something happens. The poop hits the fan, folks. I mean it gets real. Four open-heart surgeries later and that's a lot of happening. I boarded the plane anyway. "This is what normal people do," I kept telling myself. I hadn't left like this for seven years.

There I sat in my seat, adjusting to my neighbor's elbows, while the plane took off, gravity forcing me into the back of my chair. Gripping my seatbelt for dear life, I had a sudden realization: I am riding in the perfect metaphor.

I have no control of this plane. Believe me, as visions of oxygen masks dropping from the ceiling, sudden drops in cabin pressure, using my cushion as a flotation device and other lovely topics the flight attendant bubbled on about (can someone please stop her?), I knew this to the core. I just had to sit there in my seat, waiting for my 2 oz. drink to arrive and praying that the pilot wasn't drunk.

I had to surrender.

Because, this is life. And we don't know. We are not in control. We might sit by a very large man with very sharp elbows on a very tiny plane for what feels like days. We will face unexpected death and loss and grieve in a thousand different ways. But somewhere in all that surrender—if we're lucky and we make the effort—we'll find peace.

Because we're not flying the plane. That's a lot of responsibility. Take that one off your To Do List, Mama. You're not in charge. You just have to sit, with your seatbelt fastened, and enjoy the peanuts and the view.

It's beautiful, by the way, in case you have your eyes closed right now.

"And in His mercy, His grace, He gave us to each other. He made us fierce. Your bravery multiplies mine. We are a force to be reckoned with."

## May Your Basket Be Full

Whether you are a Christian or not, I believe that Easter and its messages can ring true in our lives. First, there is the sacrifice. Any parent up all night with a sick child, catching vomit in their hands, can tell you that while it wasn't fun, the efforts done in the name of love enhance the richness of life. There are few sacrifices like that of a caregiver. Selfless acts, when practiced regularly, smooth the rough surfaces of our character. I feel a closeness to my children that I wouldn't have felt had the road been easy. We take up the cross, we shoulder the burden, we give of ourselves entirely. Even if it just has symbolic meaning to you, from this vantage point, you can appreciate Jesus' sacrifice on the cross.

Also embedded in the message of Easter is rebirth—new life right now springs forth from cold winter soil. This can be the dawn of a new chapter in your life, starting fresh with new material. A springing forth of flowers from the seeds you have tended all winter.

April is also the national month for Organ Donation. Nothing says a new chance at life like a life-saving transplant. As my little girl with a little boy's heart beating in her chest runs past the tulips and stops to linger under the cherry blossoms, I thank the selfless family who chose to donate in their darkest of suffering. It is upon these heroes' shoulders that I place the mantle of hope: from death comes life, from sacrifice comes Love, we reap what has been sewn.

Love freely, friends. And buy that chick (or seven) for your kiddo. You have my permission here in writing. Consider it your next loving sacrifice.

If you become a crazy chicken lady, I'll see you at the feed store. You are welcome.

"I need someone to laugh bitterly at the irony of life with, while we eat mint-chocolate-chip ice cream and snuggle sometimes. And who would I talk about chickens or embarrass our children while we swing-dance in the kitchen? Priorities."

Humor kept us sane. Family photoshoot at the hospital, waiting for a heart, 2013

## Chapter 7

# MAWWIAGE IS WHAT BWINGS US TOGEVVER TODAY

Relationships are hard. Even with no huge bumps and giant challenges, relationships are hard. Parenting a sick child together when things get rough, is like a bull running through a china shop—things are bound to get broken. We'd been together almost 12 years before we had children (long story), and I'm grateful we had that foundation. Our china was a little tougher than many new couples. The divorce rate for families with sick kids is daunting. Often you're too busy picking up your own pieces to notice the other person isn't doing a great job either. And, standing there leaking your contents, really doesn't make for effective parenting, let alone carry the weight of running a household.

My husband and I called in a lot of artists to fill our cracks with gold—some friends, others new tools we learned to use, and some professions. And today I help other couples do the same.

I don't give advice, but the following letters generally sum up a lot of my thoughts on why we've stayed together and remained best friends through a lot of crazy. I like my husband's cracks and the way we've mended ourselves individually, coming back to what brought us together in the first place. Who else would I want to share that with? I need someone to laugh bitterly at the irony of life with, while we eat mint-chocolate-chip ice cream and snuggle sometimes. And who would I talk about chickens or embarrass our children while we swing-dance in the kitchen? Priorities.

## The Mirror is Painful

I read a statistic recently that special needs families have more than an 80% divorce rate on average and it sunk deeply. Of all the families that need a firm foundation, it's special needs families. Eric and I have not had it easy, and our marriage has been challenged on almost every front. So it has taken a lot of investment and dedication to maintain a good relationship, and most days it's not perfect.

Early on in the gritty, devastating, mess of it all, I remember seeing my partner of eleven plus years (at that time) as if he was a 6'4" tall mirror, echoing the dark, heavy, and ugly visage of my grief. Watching him walk through our home was like watching my pain take physical form and drink coffee, eat breakfast in front of me.

At the time, I could hardly handle my own sadness, let alone this constant reminder of his. Through the years, and with a lot of grace, we've navigated things pretty well. I don't give advice, because I believe that we all truly know what God is calling us to do in our relationships, but I do offer some suggestions and insights we've learned over the years that work for us (take them with a grain of salt, because we're a little odd). These are the things I might say:

1.  The currency of relationships is often appreciation and gratitude. Recognizing the good and vocalizing it as often as possible can make up for a lot of bad.

2.  You're not going to cope the same. You're not going to grieve the same. You might want to talk endlessly about your situation, he may not. Expecting different people to process all this the same isn't realistic. If one of you wants to talk more than the other, find someone else for a while to talk through things with, whether a friend or a professional. Differences on this front can create a lot of hostility and resentment.

3.  Build your toolbox. Each of you need to find healthy coping skills that fit for you individually. They won't be the same, but hopefully things overlap that you both enjoy.

4.  Protect each other's toolboxes. Give each other time and space to fill your buckets. You can't pour out of empty vessels. An ounce of prevention is worth a pound of cure here -prioritize your mental health. Trust me.

5.  Remember who you were before all this happened. Sure, things have changed, but Eriic and I frequently remind ourselves "we'd just have to find another jerk." No one is perfect, but unless there is abuse, it's often easier to recoup the love you had then to start over with single-hood, dating, dealing with someone else's baggage, and step-parenting. A marriage that has been repaired, like a seam that's been reinforced, is often stronger than the original.

6.  Keep in mind what you are focusing on. Every situation has goods and bads. Every person has goods and bads. It's up to us where we turn the spotlight.

7.  Laugh. A lot. At each other, at yourself. Humor will often save the day.

8.  You will both have a different skill set for raising your complex child. One set of skills isn't necessarily better or more important than the other. One of you may

take more of a supportive role, while the other is in the trenches. After experiencing and watching a lot of couples get resentful about a lack of balance here, I notice that we are made for certain roles in all of this.

9. I asked my husband what he felt was most important - he said that looking at each other as a "safe harbor," and choosing to protect that, learn each other's love language, shore up the foundation in your marriage and lean into whatever makes that stronger. Choose to put a pause on anything that doesn't.

10. Value your goal of leading a family through this battle over petty differences and disagreements. Rise above the small things. It builds character. If you're having trouble seeing eye to eye in a situation or decision, bring in reinforcements. Humility and a leveling of pride are some of the most important ingredients in a healthy marriage for a complex family.

"Find unity in something,
even if it's just a heartbeat."

## For Better or for Worse

I am married to my life. I have committed to my life, to love honor and cherish it, in sickness and in health, til' death do us part. But seriously, like any good marriage, I get out of it the love I put into it. Don't get me wrong—loving my life takes a massive amount of coffee, and a decent understanding of comedic irony. I have problems. My kids have problems. Even my dog has her share of problems. And don't get me started about my seriously neurotic flock of chickens.

But just last week at the height of one of my kid problems, when my life seemed just nearly unmanageable, I looked across the hospital floor at a friend's little boy's room. It suddenly occurred to me that no matter how bad things get in my life, I'm kind of attached to my own brand of problems.

After all, I'm an expert at them. I am skilled in the art of balancing the Titanic of Problems on my shoulders while doing the Praying Monkey yoga pose and sipping tea with my six-year-old. Or at least, that is how it feels at two in the afternoon when I haven't slept. I am a master at the sneak attack. Half clown, half ninja, I sneak up on those big problems in the middle of the night, then laugh at them for sucking their thumb. My problems and I, we're tight like that.

So before you try to deny you're related, like that cousin that sang bad karaoke with his fly unzipped at your wedding, remember your problems and your life are what made you a warrior. So I marry my beautiful, flawed life. For better or for worse, I embrace it for the gifts it brings. I can either commit—or be committed. It really is my choice.

PS: the same is true for my spouse. Go back, re-read, replacing the word "life" with "spouse." Don't worry, I'll wait.

"When I am truly clear, I am happy. And it has absolutely nothing to do with you. I love that I see that now. You, my dear, are the cherry on top."

## It Only Takes One

Relationships are messy. But it truly only takes one to be happy. If I question my stressful thoughts about you, I realize that my version of you shifts. I find out that what I thought happened, didn't. Suddenly I fall in love with reality. Seeing you for the first time leaves me breathless.

Byron Kaite is infamous for saying that she could walk into a busy city's street and pick any stranger off the street, and be happily married to him. Because her happiness is not dependent upon anyone. It's the exact opposite thing our culture teaches; "happy wife, happy life," right? Is it possible to *make* someone happy? Or is that their choice—my happiness, mine?

When I am truly clear, I am happy. And it has absolutely nothing to do with you. I love that I see that now. You, my dear, are the cherry on top.

## Put Down the Gloves

I don't know about you, but the people I fight with the most are the ones closest to me; the ones I love the most. Perhaps I know that no matter how vicious or biting my words get, these people will not leave. However, stepping back from it, it seems counterintuitive: shouldn't I be the most loving to the people I love the most?

I had been particularly argumentative in my marriage and it was getting old. For all of us. Flash forward to a normal Sunday. We had decided to try out a new church and the morning had already started rockily.

I held my husband's hand and prayed for something we needed to hear. What followed was magic to my heart. The pastor was speaking about the very thing that had been damaging my soul—the fighting. I had been battling many people, many things, and it did not feel good. His words came across and cut through me. He said if he had a prayer to send home with us, it would be "Lord, take the fight out of me and put the love in me." So simple.

Of course I, being a very "special" being, interpreted that as, "When you want to kill someone, sing the Love Boat theme song in a voice similar to that of a cat with the flu." It was obnoxious and it worked. Who knew???

As of writing this letter, I have not fought with a living soul since that sermon. It has been so magical, so peaceful. I surrendered the need to be right, the need to be mean, the desire to hurt anyone.

To anyone struggling (with a partner, a child, a parent, a boss): surrender to win. Put down the gloves. Let love in. Even if it means singing a cheesy sitcom theme song from the '80s.

# Chapter 8

# CRISIS COPING SKILLS (WHEN THE POOP HITS THE ROOMBA)

I'm a teacher of tools. And because of the life I've been given, I have collected a LOT of them. There is no better test of my teaching than when the rubber hits the road and I have a moment of choice as to how I handle it. The Roomba analogy comes from a hysterical story (sorry, friend) I'll tell on another day, but you can probably imagine what kind of damage Puppy Left Alone with Diarrhea on Roomba Day can create. What a metaphor for life sometimes, eh?

Crisis is a chance to test your metal. To see how solid that gold is that has been filling all your cracks. To try your tools. To let people show up. To be human. To prove your capacity, your endurance, and your strength. To surrender sometimes and crawl under the covers with a pack of Oreos.

I'm here in the mess with you, Mama.

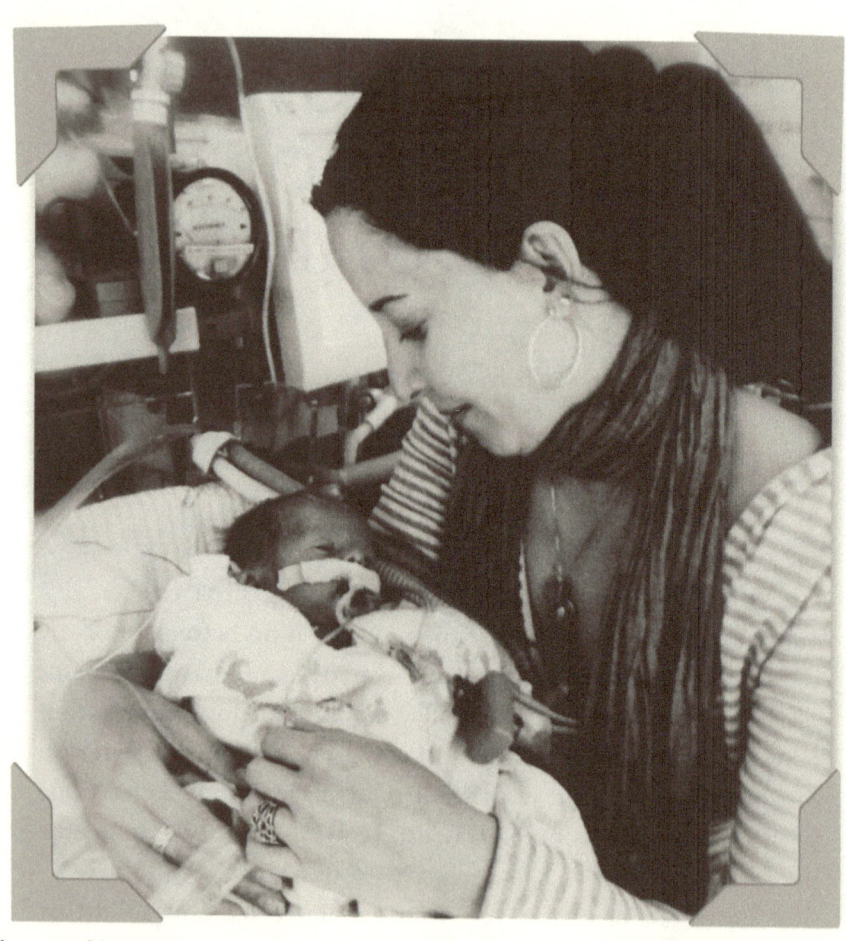

*"Holding" my baby for the first time after her first surgery. About 2 wks old. 2011*

## First Aid for the Heart

When I became pregnant with my first daughter, I received my first union card for the League of Worry, the union that every parent joins. Even though Juna was safe inside my belly, I began to worry about raising the child to whom I hadn't even given birth yet.

One of my many worries was addiction. Eric and I have it on both sides of our family, and I have seen the wreckage it causes as parents struggle to contain a teenager bent on self-destruction. I (perhaps mistakenly) thought it was in my power to prevent addictive behavior by parenting well. Ah, the first-time Mom delusions.

I had a very good family friend who had run a treatment center downtown for more than 25 years, so I went to visit him. I asked him for advice. He said to me, "I don't know what you can do as a parent, but I can tell you this: every single person who has ever walked through the door of this treatment center has lacked Healthy Coping Skills."

The way I cope with the range of human emotion we go through, really indicates my spiritual health. And what I have learned over the years is that everyone has different things that help them regulate emotion—there is no one-size-fits-all Spiritual Toolkit.

When we were waiting in the hospital for my daughter's heart transplant, and every open-heart surgery before it, I was under a lot of emotional stress and turmoil. Many parents in my position went home from the hospital to a glass (or three) of wine. Because of my liver disease, this was not a remote possibility. And smoking wasn't an option either. Neither tool would've served me anyway. I needed healthy ways to Cope (with a capital C) the war being waged in my life.

A sick child put my Spiritual Toolkit to use. I took baths, I wrote a book, I exercised, I took walks, I wrote some more, I did yoga, I drank chamomile tea, I called my best friend to vent and cry, I cleaned. These are the healthy things that help me get through difficult times without making unhealthy choices. There are other things like books, movies, etc., but when they are used as an escape method, it is very temporary. Emotions are like four-year old children: if they don't get attention and the necessary addressing of an issue, they will tug on your pant leg until they do get some kind of resolution. Sometimes they tug for years until therapy is the best course of treatment. Sometimes they have a meltdown in Aisle 7 of the grocery store if you ignore them long enough.

As harsh as it sounds, we only have ourselves (and God) on this journey. Much like we take care of our body, our spirits must be cared for and nurtured too. What good is it for the body to survive when the spirit is so damaged that one can't even have peace in the life they are living?

Cheers to finding your First Aid kit—treat your heart and soul with the kindness it deserves. I'd suggest ginger beer. Trust me.

## The Heart of the Artichoke

In 2011 I survived a war. Read, fetal echoes, grief, ICUs, surgeries, medications, complications, so many complications, a laundry list of frightening stories and what-ifs a mile long that kept me up at night. Nowadays I regularly say in my writings, "Don't get all future-y, Mama," and boy was I in that unknown and terrifying future those many years ago. It lay before me like a minefield I had to cross, with a sick baby on my hip the whole way.

At night, I drove home with the sirens of the ICU still beeping in my ears, to the rest of my family. We were divided in so many ways. Because I couldn't clone myself, I was never in the right place. Seven months of that. Seven long months before I took my baby home, and I arrived on that doorstep broken. More surgeries lay ahead. More breaking. I felt fragile.

But my husband was more broken, so I did what I do and I signed him up for a therapist. After the first session, he came home with a book. "Loving What Is" by Byron Katie. I passed it off as some crunchy woo-woo that this new therapist was selling and I went about my life, still damaged, but breathing. I think I was perhaps born cynical.

But before my eyes, he changed. He changed a lot. Weeks went by and he was...just...freer. I started sneaking glances over his shoulder at night while we lay in bed, of this book. What was this catalyst for change? Was it some kind of voodoo? I had to see for myself.

So I went to his therapist. And together we started doing The Work. And it WAS magical. Years of therapy never moved mountains like this Work did. The process, simple, empowering, portable. She simply helped me question stressful beliefs that I had previously subscribed to like the daily newspaper. Stressful thoughts had become the hell between my ears. I wanted heaven again.

Over the dozen years since, this inquiry, this Work, slowly unraveled all of it. Like the most delicious but prickly artichoke. Slowly peeling away the rough layers, gradually over the years, a continual process, my leaves became softer, until hopefully I arrive at the golden heart.

I questioned grief.

I questioned suffering.

I questioned death.

I questioned the traumas of my past.

I questioned beliefs about you, beliefs about me.

I questioned everything.

Until nothing was left but my freedom: absolute peace. Love, acceptance, and gratitude. So much gratitude. Years later, and I love this life I have been given. And if that changes, I simply do the Work and I love what is again.

And now I get to share it. Lift the water, all boats rise. Life can be hard. Suffering is optional.

"And that's all we can do.
Don't let the 'what-ifs' drag you
down, Mama. You'll miss the magic
of the moment."

## The What-Ifs Will Drag You Down

The average lifetime of a pediatric heart transplant is 10-15 years. I know children that have died at the age of four, and young women who are 20+ years out and doing fine. She's several years out from transplant and the truth is simple: we just don't know how much time we have with her.

How does that fact not leave me curled in the fetal position on my closet floor? Mama, if you're like me, you need to fight to stay present. This is what I do on a regular basis:

I take pictures. I mean, craploads of pictures. I push her on the swing. I jump with her on the tramp. I hold her every night while she goes to sleep and wake her with kisses every morning. I make plastic cup vases of all the flowers she collects for me on our walks. I hang her scribbled paintings on the wall. I overcome my germophobia and send her to school because she loves it. I send her with yummy lunches and always a cookie. I play dress-up. I read her any book she brings me and more. I say "I love you" 50 times a day. I relish giving her medicine regularly and oxygen when she needs it. The fact is, there are hundreds of mothers out there that wish they could do even one of these things for their child who is gone.

And I know in my heart, that if I ever become one of those mothers, I'll have used the time I had with this angel on Earth, however long or short it is, in the best way possible. I can't afford to take her for granted.

And that's all we can do. Don't let the "what-ifs" drag you down, Mama. You'll miss the magic of the moment.

"But if you get lost in the tangled dark thoughts, worry becomes the THIEF that robs you of the moment."

First year of preschool, almost 4 years old, 2015

## Mama, You're Missing the Good Part

You, hovering in the dark, your face lit by the glow of numbers of her pulse-ox, STOP—you're missing the miracle of her breathing, the softness of her cheek as she sighs, the rise and fall of her little chest. It's a miracle she's even alive, isn't it?

Earlier, while you looked at the paleness of her skin, the swelling in her face, wondering if you heard her cough, you missed the original artwork with jelly fingerprints that she was proudly showing you. You didn't really see it at all, did you?

You dropped her off for her first day of preschool, and in the middle of the will-she-be-okay-without-me-ness of the moment, you missed how excited and scared she was. You forgot to memorize the warmth of her hand in yours before you said goodbye.

It's easy to get lost in the fog of worry. You're a walking medical historian, and you feel like it all rests with you. What a weight you carry. Looking in the mirror lately though, you see a stranger. You look so old. So damaged.

But what if you dropped it?

What if you played hooky the next day you were supposed to stand guard? Tomorrow. What if you just held her hand, blew dandelions, and pushed her on the swing as if the two of you didn't have a care in the world?

Breathe in that freedom, Mama.

Because life is precarious for all of us. But if you get lost in the tangled dark thoughts, Worry becomes the THIEF that robs you of the moment. Stop getting all future-y, Mama. You're both alive right now. Breathing. It's a freaking miracle.

Remember joy? I know you do. Live in that instead.

## When I See Clearly

A week ago, I was an emotional wreck.

Because today is a big day. There are so many ways I could approach my daughter's annual heart biopsy (they go into her femoral artery with a catheter, to measure pressure, look at coronaries and take a piece of her heart to test for rejection). So many options and ways to handle this. The choice is always mine. My first instinct is anxiety—fear of the unknown. I think of all the unhappy endings around me, mothers who have received bad news or even lost children in similar situations. My brain turns into a two-year-old having a temper tantrum stomping my feet and balling my fists "I don't WANT to take her in!!"

What an ugly place to dwell. And painful.

The truth is, that when I go in that state of mind, I am not present for my daughter. I suffer. Is she suffering? No. She lives in the present. She played all week, and now she is blissfully asleep with anesthesia. While I wait with a pager on my hip and a latte in my hand (I didn't eat breakfast out of solidarity).

So I put my feet up in the waiting room without my story of a pager going off too early. I simply watch the movie unfold. I meet with doctors who may or may not deliver news they think is bad. Or good. I try my best to love it all. There is no wrong way to do it. There is only peace or no peace. Without my story, I am waiting for one of the loves of my life to be served by her doctors. Nothing more.

Don't get me wrong—it's work. But it's a lot harder to suffer. That's my experience, at least.

A simple four-step process helped save my own heart. I'll see you on the other side of my news today.

## Nothing Is Under Control

You're about to find out why I needed to invent Posilution®. And yes, I know it's an old concept with a new name. To me, it was CPR. "Posilution®" is the training of the mind to see everything in a positive light. It is short for the "Positive Revolution" and creating it, then learning to do it was indeed the revolution that this heart mom desperately needed, but I'll get to why (and how) in another book. Using it in my practice, one can practically watch someone's neuro-pathways change radically. I watched my life improve. It's a guarantee. It is the very reason I am not in a padded room with a tight-fitting white blazer right now, actually. It is life. And I'll tell you why I needed it.

These are just a few of my worries on a DAILY basis (sometimes hourly) before I used Posilution®: Is she happy? Did she get her meds? Is she sniffling? Has she taken in enough calories? When is her next lab draw? Will they get her on the first poke or will it take many like usual? How is she going to survive this emotionally? Is she going to live? Am I going to be a grieving Mom? Is that my destiny? How will Juna live without her? How will we all live without her? How will we live without her magic? Is she happy? How does her echo look? Is her kidney function improving now? Has she had enough to eat today? How am I going to get her to eat vegetables? Will she make it to Junior HIgh? Will she have a first crush? What about high school? What about that massive radiation exposure? Will we be visiting the cancer ward next? Will she get the chance to fall in love? How long will that precious heart last? Should she be getting more exercise? Will that help? Is that kid over there sick? I think I heard him cough. Would it help to spray her in Lysol? Should she be wearing a mask to preschool? How is she going to emotionally survive this? Is she broken? How are her kidneys? Are we a match because I'll give her mine? Will she go to college? Will she live? I am so attached please God I can't do this. Is she happy? Did she get her meds? Why is she so used to all these needle pokes? Why is she so used to pain? Is she going to live? Will I get to be at her wedding? Will her Daddy get to walk her down that aisle? What can I do that I'm not doing? What more can I do? What have I missed?

It leaves me breathless every dang day. But there is an answer.

The only answers that I've ever found are in Posilution® and staying present. I've stopped believing I can pray hard enough to change it. She wouldn't have a new heart if that were true. So I try to keep moving forward and staying in the present with my precious girl. Nothing is in my control, but I can surrender to reality, God's plan, being better for me than my own way. And

I can Posilute® enough to remain happy. Because that is the best gift I can give my delicate warrior. I'll fight by her side, and I will do it with a smile. And I'll be grateful for every single day I get.

I love lemons. Because they are gifts. Hardship has given me so much more than "Easy" ever did. Go out and love those lemons, they are growing you beautifully.

## Stay in the Moment, Mama.

Her future is uncertain. Her life, tenuous. I could dwell on the unknown, dark and dangerous expanse before us. I could picture it looming large above me like a dense boulder held by a skinny rope and pulley, frayed, hanging over our heads. I have a funny picture in my head of Wile E. Coyote's anvil and rope over the road runner. Who knows when it may fall? Often, like the coyote, I get trapped under my own anvil.

But the gift she has given me (oh there are so many) is to dwell in the moment. Notice the tendrils of hair brushing my neck. Feel the weight of her warm body. Notice that I can feel her heart if I get still enough. Notice that in this moment, it is beating—strong, fierce, sure and steady. I take this moment because it is all I have.

Feel the perfection of this very minute: we are given all we need. The idea of a future makes me smile. How silly is it for me to dwell there in that unknown darkness when this moment is just so perfect? God gave it to us.

## What Door Are You Pushing Against?

Trying to change something for days, weeks, months, years, sometimes a lifetime, can be absolutely exhausting. Frustrating. Mind-numbing. It's like trying to get into a building that you really want to get in (something great and desirable is inside that building). And there you are, leaning against the door, two hands pressing, all your body weight and energy pressed against this door, and it won't budge. This door doesn't push to open. In your heart, you may know this, but you REALLY want in that building!

Imagine spending weeks, months, years, leaning everything into that door.

Fighting the reality of that test result.

Trying to make your mother less toxic.

Trying to make your husband really listen.

Trying to get your son to make good choices.

Fighting the diagnosis.

Trying to change the alcoholic.

Hoping the abuse will stop.

Questioning the unfairness of death, sickness, loss.

Waiting for that apology.

What if you stopped pushing? Step back. Look at that door. Notice how exhausted your body is from pushing all this time.

Take a breath. Notice. Accept that the door doesn't open by pushing it. See that door for what it is.

Suddenly you have options. More energy. Does this door pull to open? Can you go in through the window? Is there another entrance?

Is this a building you EVEN WANT TO GO IN? Perhaps you've been pushing for years trying to enter this building, and you don't even know what's inside or if it's what you want anymore. Habits can keep you stuck.

It might seem ridiculous, this image of someone pushing on a door for years, and sometimes we just have to laugh at our humanness. "Insanity is trying the same thing over and over again, expecting different results."—Albert Einstein

Surrender. Stop pushing. Accept that door for what it is. Breathe. Watch the opportunities open up. God wants you to see something here. What is it?

"No one can pour from an empty vessel. 'Self-care' has been a trend sometimes looked down upon as hedonistic and selfish. Yet for the parents carrying it all, self-care is vital. What happens to the ship when the captain goes down?"

## Medical Mama, Heal Thyself

Yes, we are strong. Yes we are made for this battle. Yes, we make sacrifices, and work hard, and advocate, and cry in the shower where no one can hear us, and yes, we talk to doctors with medical degrees longer than our arms and say, "No, not for my child," and yes, we hold miracles, we beg for their lives, we schedule therapies and procedures, we scrub our baby's chests the night before they are cut open, we hold their hands and pray they wake up, we beg on our knees, we hope for their future, we schedule our vacations around the nearest hospital, we weigh the risks and the benefits of hot tubs and swimming pools and preschools and lakes and chickens and shots, and medicine, so much medicine.

We give so much. So much.

Yet when we hear on the plane, "Put the oxygen on yourself before helping others with theirs," we don't seem to think this applies to our own lives. Who has the time for that?

"Right?" I say, clinging on to my sanity like it's the last parachute with two of us left on the plane.

We spend so much time helping our kids to live, but forget that we, too, are supposed to enjoy this life. What if you worried less? What if you saw that next surgery as hopeful instead of dreadful? What if you saw transplant as a blessing and not a failed surgery? What if you just felt...less stressed, less worried, less bitter, less exhausted? What if you had great coping skills to show off? Wouldn't that ALSO help your child?

It's my passion to support the child through the parents. Our kids' therapists spend an hour with them a week, and we spend the other 167, but yet it's the child who needs the help? Support the parent, help the child. No one can pour from an empty vessel. "Self-care" has been a trend sometimes looked down upon as hedonistic and selfish. Yet for the parents carrying it all, self-care is vital. What happens to the ship when the captain goes down?

Blessings to you on this bumpy road. Perhaps finally getting help for yourself is the 253rd and final wind you needed. Living room doctor, heal thyself.

Shiloh, Mimi, Juna in Boston, 2013 (Mimi stayed with us for 2 months here)

## When People Don't Show Up to Help You Climb That Mountain or "Grace for the Couch Potato."

Friends absent? Family not showing up? People not understanding? Feeling abandoned and alone on that mountain you're climbing?

I've worked through this myself and with tons of families in my coaching practice. The process I use really simplifies this for me, and here's what I've come to find. Hopefully through hearing the results of my inner investigations, you can find the truth for you.

1.  The right people show up. Sure there were people who completely disappeared when the poop hit the fan, and it hurt. But through my therapeutic work, I found that those people didn't have the capacity. Would you ask a kindergartener to climb Mount Kilimanjaro? Seems ridiculous, but why would I expect someone who isn't capable to show up in the way I need? It is very human to be uncomfortable with illness and death. Consider it a "fitness level." Some people aren't mentally fit enough to hold the hard stuff. The people who can are gifted. Please note that this knowledge is not a weapon. "You obviously aren't capable" is hurtful and only deepens wounds. Having quiet understanding and compassion keeps your side of the road clean. Appreciate those that have the capacity. Not many have it, but wow, what a blessing when you encounter those that do, right when you need it. I'm grateful for the gift that God gave me to run towards crises, not away. I'm pretty certain I got it from my mother, the best "Mimi" in the world, who set aside her life for two months to live with us in Boston. But it's not everyone's gift. And not everyone is gifted with a mom like her. Other "moms" show up, though.

2. People who haven't experienced it truly can't understand. Expecting people to "get it" is a lost cause. That's why there are support groups with common struggles. I look to friends for surface-level understanding, basic parenting stuff, the best hike for kids, when my husband won't do the dishes, basic. I rely on heart moms to understand heart mom stuff. The truth is, only you and God *truly* get your exact experience. Even your child's experience differs from yours. Expecting others to understand is unrealistic, and that's why it hurts. I explain this to my daughter quite a bit; how can one know what an onion tastes like until they've tasted it? Patience and compassion for these folks is the way to go; lower your expectations. There are good people who want to understand—people who want to hear about your mountain or even try to climb some of it with you—I've learned to appreciate those kind souls. Still, it's just me and God in the end who truly know my footsteps.

3. People don't know what to say. I had a good friend just disappear, and it was shocking and hurtful. When I asked her what happened, I learned that she and her husband were struggling (ah it's not just me going through life and climbing mountains) and she also "didn't know what to say." This was a giving, generous person. Sometimes what you're going through is so horrendous that people are afraid to do or say the wrong thing. Look at their intention, not the outcome. The height of that mountain is terrifying. They truly just have to love and pray from afar until you show them what you need. ("Just come and sit with me, take me to coffee and let's talk about nothing, let's go to a movie and binge-eat ice cream.") Sometimes you need to tell people it's okay to cheer your climb on in other ways.

4. Your journey will be awkward for people. I had to ask a new neighbor and mom friend yesterday if their family had had stomach flu in the last week (our kryptonite). I mean, *AWKWARD* health screening from a stranger. Moms don't feel they can complain about teething when your baby is sitting there with a feeding tube. Comparing your lives, either out loud, or internally, can push people away unintentionally. The disconnect in understanding creates distance, and that sucks. People don't understand, but again, expecting them to is unrealistic. I've learned not to talk about certain things at parties—LOL "hey let's talk about PTLD or the Year-Long Stomach Flu" have been topics I awkwardly navigated in the past. No one gets it and it creates distance. Find your crowd for that.

Most times our friends and family do what they can. Maybe this kindergartener can walk a mile, or do jumping jacks, but they're not trained for that 5-mile uphill hike yet. Meet people on their level. I've learned to have empathy for those that can't know, can't show up. This journey has taught me how to show up, and I'm grateful for that. It has made me fit for the big climbs.

"This journey is a beautiful sifting and shifting. The mountain can be lonely and treacherous. Hopefully you can find your people and adjust your expectations of those who still love you, but can't understand, and can't do more than watch you climb. Love those couch potatoes anyway."

## Grace for the Couch Potato 2.0

You are climbing a big mountain.

Some people will stand at the bottom and hope you make it safely, watching, praying.

Some people won't be able to watch.

Others won't think you're climbing it well, or shouldn't climb it at all.

And some, very few, will try to climb it with you.

But only you and God experience ALL those steps, those stumbles, those victories.

Expecting others to understand climbing the exact same mountain is unrealistic and painful.

Appreciating those that do what they can, is Grace.

And some parts, you may have to walk alone with only God's understanding.

It's hard having things like this affect your friendships. Again, the right people show up. My brother didn't meet my daughter 'til she was 3, and he lived 15 minutes away. Yet a neighbor came twice a week to the hospital to sit with her—a "better" brother than I was born with. I've found compassion for my brother (he just wasn't in shape to climb that mountain with me), and deep gratitude for that neighbor who climbed part of it with me.

This journey is a beautiful sifting and shifting. The mountain can be lonely and treacherous. Hopefully you can find your people, and adjust your expectations of those who still love you, but can't understand, and can't do more than watch you climb. And love those couch potatoes anyway, through their fragility–often they are climbing mountains you aren't even aware of, and are stronger in ways you can't be.

I hope you stop sometimes and look back and feel the joy of the summit.

# Re-sil-ience

Noun.

1. the capacity to recover quickly from difficulties; toughness.

2. the ability of a substance or object to spring back into shape; elasticity

In all your wars, Mama, when beaten to your knees, in utter desperation and surrender, did you ever feel your bones that held you? Did you feel the floor as it rose up against you, supporting you in your anguish, your grief?

In the midst of struggle, we need a measuring stick, an odometer, to keep us aware of all we've come through, all we've survived. That mileage on you may have added a few worry lines and gray hairs, but feel how strong your engine has become. You are a survivor, Mama. You've weathered the storms.

And you've carried a sick child with you the whole way.

And that frail little bird that keeps you up at night? She has weathered the storm too. She's got your strength, your grit, your survival skills too. Sure, we're all a little worn for the wear, but we are proofed in the fire, like steel, made stronger through these challenges, these trials. Our hearts continue to beat, our lungs take in the air, our body is an engine with fuel to burn. We were given this road to travel, and when we take a moment to look up, the scenery we pass is gorgeous.

Stop for a moment, even if you feel alone in all this, take in that beauty, that grit, that drive of yours. It is fuel.

Let no one question your strength, your resilience. Let it shine from you. Know that with each battle you face, you have survived others, you will survive more. This engine is strong, the ground will hold you.

Let the road you travel, the miles you endure, make you better, not bitter. Mama, you and that little bird of yours are made of strong stuff. Wipe the road-weary dust off your brow and smile—you were made for this. This fine-tuned engine of yours?

It hums.

## *Trigger Warning:* Bulletproof Ponytails

"Jennifer, you hurt Mary's feelings when you teased her! See what you did? Look at her crying. Now, apologize."

Sound familiar? Our culture, from a very young age, teaches us to take responsibility for each other's feelings. Teaches us that we can control others' reactions to what we say and do. Teaches us that others can take us hostage, can actually force us to feel and react in certain ways to what they say, what they do, and how they say and do it.

They triggered me. Is this really possible?

Can you literally step into someone's mind and body and initiate tears, anger? Pull a lever, create a chemical, take over their nervous system, physically make them cry, decide for them that their feelings are hurt? Initiate memories of their childhood abandonment issues? Direct their brain back to that moment 10 years ago? Define who they are for them? Control how they interpret your words, your body language?

It is physically impossible to control someone else's emotions and reaction.

Which is why it feels impossible not to offend someone. It seems impossible to protect someone's feelings enough. We've invented the art of leapfrogging, side-stepping, language-crafting, and *emotional parkour* to keep from offending or hurting others when it's absolutely impossible! Their reaction is their choice.

And what a powerless feeling to be on the other side—being at the mercy of everything someone says—waiting with bated breath to hear someone say the wrong word to send us spinning into emotional turmoil. No space is safe enough. We've absolutely surrendered our power.

IT IS MY CHOICE how I react to what you say and do. I take back that power! I am not a victim. The ironic story is that the company I originally approached with the design of this book, ripped my ideas and mockups to shreds. If I had run to my safe space, I would have lost out on the best book cover designer in the business. Instead, I decided not to take it personally and listen to feedback. He truly wanted the best outcome for me.

Yes, it's ideal that people are kind. Yes, respect and decency are important. I can still set boundaries and remind people to be kind, but it is their choice how they move in the world. That is something that each person has to live with in themselves. But I'm certainly not going to surrender my emotional well-being to someone who doesn't make that choice. They don't have that power, and I'm not going to give it to them.

We need to undo this cultural expectation that others "keep us safe." Not only is it physically impossible, there is no power in that! I choose my feelings! I choose who I surround myself with! I am in charge of my body and my reactions! This fragility isn't helping us—because it simply isn't physically possible. Even worse, it's creating an identity of victimhood. There is no power in victimhood. We've invented entire language constructs, banned words, put up signs to avoid offending each other, and it simply isn't possible. There will always be something more to trigger us if we're looking for it. If we aren't emotionally resilient.

We are handing over all our power when we blame others for our feelings and reactions. We, as parents of complex children, have enough trauma.

We can own our emotions and we can still set boundaries. We can learn what brings people closer and what drives people away. We can speak our truth, and we can keep our side of the road clean by speaking with as much respect as possible. We can sit with our hurt and anger and offense until we're ready to change our perspective and heal ourselves. We can look to God as the one being who truly understands instead of expecting it from others. We can believe in ourselves, stand up for ourselves, brush things off, get back up again, stronger this time. That's resilience. That's power.

And nothing that Jennifer says or does can touch Mary.

That is Bulletproof.

The pure joy of sisterhood. Juna (5) and Shiloh (3). 2014

## I'd Watch "The Good News at Six"

People wonder why I don't watch the news. It's simple: I want to be happy. Perspective is everything in life—our thoughts and experiences color everything—and I want to see the world as crime-free and beautiful. The only bad thing that has ever happened from not watching is that I've missed daylight savings time twice. Small price to pay for peace in my opinion. People object to that, saying it's Pollyanna. "The world is burning, Hilary, and you're focusing on the fact that you're warm and toasty." Nope.

Every situation has Dark and Light. Every one. I've tested this, but please send me an email if you've found an exception. Fires. Birth, Death. Heart defects. Cancer. Everything. So if we are holding the spotlight, where do we aim it? Focusing on the positive in a situation actually helps us navigate life better. Study after study shows that more optimistic kids become more successful adults. Because when they encounter hardship, they have hope for a way around. They endure. They overcome.

I hear people talking about "end of days" and how horrible and dangerous the world is and it hurts my heart. We see the world like this because of media, social and otherwise. We just hear more about awful crimes that happen and that is the only difference. Media loves to dramatize and sensationalize crime (because iit sells), so we hear about one instance for weeks, sometimes years. It colors our vision, and it is unfortunate because it's untrue. Yes there is a lot of evil in this world. In my eyes, evil wins when it takes over our minds and colors our perception of the world. There is so much goodness sprouting everywhere, even in the most difficult of situations and struggling communities. In fact, according to Time Magazine, crime in the U.S. at least, is at an all-time low in decades when this book came out! Lighten up your load, my fellow humans—the world is a friendly place. Choose to see it.

# Chapter 9

# HOLDING THE HEAVY

I had a client once tell me, "There are two kinds of people—those who run away from the hard stuff, and those who run toward it." I've been gifted with the ability to run. I enjoy deep conversations about hard stuff (which is why I'm so fun at parties). I like wading through deep waters, helping people hold their grief, untangling the emotions to find the lesson in the suffering. The Buddhists say life is suffering. I say life is suffering, BUT we have a way to go beyond that, to feel God, to grow, to let our storms carve us into more beautiful versions of ourselves.

I like helping people to fill their own cracks with gold. I'm not a healer, I'm a teacher. When I create something myself, I own it. I cherish the gold that fills my own cracks. I teach people the art of kintsugi. They become artisans. It takes bravery.

"Yes, You will rise from the ashes, But the burning comes first. For this part, Darling, You must be brave." — **Kalen Dion.**

The lamb who sat with Shiloh when I couldn't be there in the evenings.

## Nursing the Heartbreak

I bought a stuffed lamb that plays lullabies and womb sounds when she was still in my belly, when I learned her heart was sick. At two days old, I left her in a surgeon's hands. Visiting her after surgery, seeing her on all those machines keeping her alive, I placed the lamb in her isolette and turned to the nurse.

"I have a two-year-old at home, so I won't always be here. Will you play the heartbeat in this lamb while I'm gone? She might hear it and think it's mine. It'll be all she has of me. Please." With tears in her eyes, the nurse said yes.

Each nurse finished his or her shift every 12 hours, and passed on in report, vital signs and IV meds, and careful instructions to play the lamb for my baby when I was not there.

Back home, torn between two worlds, I looked out the window while my two-year-old played. Rain came down. I wondered to myself if the lamb might be playing the sound of a heart breaking. Each time I walked back into the ICU, there was my lamb—playing my heartbeat.

A nurse had decided my baby needed a little bow glued to her head, so my lamb held the safety pin with all the bows as these nurses "dressed" my baby in the only thing that would fit around all those tubes and cords and IVs trailing from her tiny 5-pound body: a tiny little bow. They played lullabies for her. They touched her when I could not.

And 24 days after I left my baby in the hands of a surgeon, I was able to hold her again and it was a nurse who made that possible too. A nurse cried with me when she told me I couldn't take my baby home for Christmas three months later. And a nurse was cheering three months after that when I finally got to take her home, along with a generous amount of home medical equipment and a healthy dose of sheer terror. Nurse, you passed the baton to a home health nurse who held my hand and showed ME how to be a nurse to one little girl.

That nurse also left my living room to run out to the car to phone my pediatrician, by the way, to tell the doctor that a child that sick should not be in my living room, or any living room for that matter. "I trust Hilary," the doctor said. So God bless the doctors that believe home is healing too. And thank you to that nurse that came back in the house and supported me while I nursed my baby back to health.

Thank you to all the nurses who helped raise my delicate baby. Who loved her when I was not there. Your tenderness helped heal my own heart, too.

"We sometimes lose our children, and the piece that is torn from us leaves a hole so big we think it might swallow us up. Sometimes it does for a while. But I've learned that the heart does grow back. Endlessly, it seems. It might be a little tattered, a little worse for wear, but it is there. Just changed, transformed, illuminated."

## Take Another Little Piece of My Heart

They are taking a piece of my daughter's heart today, sending it off to a lab somewhere. We'll see if it comes back for rejection. Waiting for her in the waiting room seems like an eternity. Oh tiny, red, and fleshy magic eight ball: what is our fate?

I know what it's like—to lose a piece of your heart. It happened the first day I became a parent. My baby wasn't breathing normally. Ah, parenthood—what a gut-wrenching initiation it can be.

The first piece of my heart.

And later, so many huge decisions. My second baby had something wrong with her heart, even as she was still in my belly. I chose to fight, to put another chunk of my heart on the line. Later, I held her, my arms wrapped tight, protectively, shielding her as the bombs in the ICU went off. And yet, the sun shined outside. No one knew I was missing pieces, so many pieces. I even managed to smile. Ah, resilience.

They've taken so many pieces of my daughter's heart since her transplant that I've lost count. Yet, no one knows out in the world, in her school, at the gymnastics school, in the pizza parlor, that she's missing a part of her heart, either.

As parents, we kiss wounds, we cringe when a bully wins in the schoolyard, we fight battles big and small. We sometimes lose our children, and the piece that is torn from us leaves a hole so big we think it might swallow us up. Sometimes it does for a while.

But here's the thing.

I have learned something big in my four plus decades that defies all that science teaches us: the heart does grow back. Endlessly, it seems. It might be a little tattered, a little worse for wear, but it is there. Just, changed, transformed, illuminated. And what is even better to me, is that if there were lab results we could read from every piece of my heart that's ever been taken, they'd say that I've transformed a little too.

So, Life, take another little piece of my heart. You know you will. I offer it to you freely. It's called parenthood.

Signed,

Just another parent in the waiting room, hoping.

## Deep Waters

Mama, it can be easy to take your darkest moments and want to stuff them in a compartment far far away never to see the light of day. But if you have nothing to judge the good moments by, where is your measure?

Embrace the difficult, dark times in your life, Mama. Put a sad song on the radio, wrap your arms around your tired body, and sway to that sound. Marinate in that deep blue gift.

These deep waters are wearing away your rough spots. Carving you like the sacred rock canyons. They don't define you—your reaction to them does.

You can choose to be better or bitter, Mama. Until then, hold on and sway.

And when the waters dry, when the sun shines on your path, you will suddenly see how far you have come. Walk to the mirror. Drink in your visage. See triumph, see joy, see growth. You have gone deeper than most. What perspective you have on life, Mama. You truly know the dark and can judge the power of the light. See joy. Drink in that deep gratitude, that triumph that only warriors at the end of battle know.

And when darkness comes again—because it will—have proof that light is possible. Have proof of your strength, your resilience, your victories big and small. You are wondrous.

You are made better by these deep waters, Mama. See that.

## The Other Shoe

Four and a half years ago, I was inducted into the sorority of worry. It happened years ago when I first became a parent to some extent, but it was nothing compared to our second daughter's diagnosis at 19 weeks in utero that her heart was critically ill.

I've endured seeing my daughter's chest opened four times. I've watched her fight to live. I've fought endless battles in and out of the hospital. Most days I feel like I am holding the Titanic on my shoulders and I'm getting tired. Luckily for me, most days I'm also able to carry that burden with a smile on my face. I even laugh.

The most common question I get from people who learn about her transplant is, "How long will her heart last?" Followed closely by, "Does it grow with her?" Yes, it grows with her. The first question is unanswerable. I will try to answer it, though, by telling you that I know a beautiful young woman 25 years out from a heart transplant, waiting for a kidney, but doing pretty well. I also know two seven-year-olds on their second heart transplants. The average is 10-15 years, but odds mean nothing. A successful heart transplant is a crap shoot—it all depends on the heart your child is blessed to get and what their body chooses to do with it. What that means for my daughter is anyone's guess. For now, it means a second chance at life—we're so grateful. I feel blessed to have the small amount of complications we've had. So lucky so far.

Most days I am present. Byron Katie taught me that if I want depression, I can get a past and if I want anxiety, I can get a future. There just isn't a lot of power in me to do anything about either. So I focus on now, quality, not quantity of life, and we live and love.

Every few months or so, though, the darkness looming in the distance whispers to me, waking me up to the reality of future possibilities: heart failure, another transplant, perhaps worse. In those moments, I get tired of waiting for the other shoe to drop. Most days I try to focus on and enjoy the bliss of a sweet life with her alive—smiling and giggling and enjoying school. But there are days that all the chocolate in the world doesn't cut it.

So here's your assignment ("wait, Hilary, I didn't know this book came with *homework?I*"): find another parent of a medically-fragile child and hug them. Most likely if you pass them in the hall at school in the morning, you'll have no idea the night they had. Hug and laugh deeply with them—it's the only cure for the endless wait for the other shoe—for both of you.

"But as it does, life dragged me there. Transplant was not what I wanted for my daughter. But OH, when I look back on what it gave us… Independence Day has a whole new meaning. Sometimes life drags you where you should be."

## Independence Day

Years ago, I was traveling across the country with a toddler in heart failure. She screamed the whole plane ride. My screaming was all internal. Why do we resist life?

The surgery that was supposed to change her life was the very thing that was threatening it—I hadn't realized that yet. We landed, and at home that night, surrounded by friends and family, we watched fireworks exploding. The smell of smoke in the air—we felt safe—ignorant, and blissful. I felt free that night.

Just days later we were in a hospital again, and in just a handful of weeks, we were waiting for a heart. Behind us, there were more surgeries, more lab draws, more IVs, more procedures, than any toddler should have. In two short years, a war. And she was a fighter.

And so was I—transplant was not what I wanted for my daughter. I fought hard.

But as it does, life dragged me there. Three months later, inpatient in the hospital, in and out of the ICU, watching my baby get sicker, a family said yes and I was in shock. So torn between gratitude and grief, it was almost as if I was in the room with that other mommy when she said goodbye to her son for the last time. He was four.

Transplant is not easy. But today, my daughter runs. She goes to summer camp. She is in gymnastics. She hikes. She swims. She giggles on the swing as I push her, watching her blond hair flying in the sun. She is learning to read, and she sings like a little songbird.

Transplant was not what I wanted for my daughter. But OH, when I look back on what it gave us, Independence Day has a whole new meaning.

Sometimes life drags you where you should be.

## National Donate Life Month

We drove into the sunrise on October 11, 2013, our wedding anniversary. The call we'd been waiting for had woken us at 6 AM. I remember it vividly—the sky, a lemonade pink as we drove to our baby's home on the hill. The drive was bittersweet. We were on our way to that hospital to say goodbye to the heart that had struggled to keep our daughter alive the last two years. We rode in silence knowing that we were driving because someone's precious child had died. And these parents, in the moment of their deepest grief, had said "yes" to saving a stranger. We were in shock—it was almost too much to comprehend.

Our daughter Shiloh had been born with a critical heart defect, surviving three open-heart surgeries before she was a year and a half old. The last surgery had failed her, and she was emergently listed for a heart transplant on August 14, 2013. We waited 88 days in the hospital for that life-saving call. It was our only hope. I watched, day after day, as my sweet toddler got sicker before my eyes. She could barely endure her 2nd birthday party, held in a conference room on the fourth floor.

We were saved by that call in the nick of time only a week later. Our daughter's sick heart would not have lasted much longer.

Then, two weeks after her transplant, I wrote a letter to our donor family to express our unending gratitude. Our two families had been married in the most beautiful, heartbreaking, miraculous way. I have never loved strangers so much. I heard back from them three months later. They told me of their son Silas, a four-year-old who was their only child and their biggest joy. The last words his mother whispered to him were, "You are my sunshine." It felt like no coincidence that this was the same song I had sung Shiloh to sleep with for her entire life. It gave me comfort that Silas's heart would hear it again.

That little boy's heart has done incredibly well for Shiloh. It was such a perfect match. We strive each day to honor their gift by living life to the fullest and taking the best care of our little girl and her precious new heart.

We live every day since her transplant in gratitude. As you can imagine, Shiloh was born with a lot of fight in her, and her feisty, unique personality captures everyone's heart. Recently she said to me "Mama, the kids all ask me why I sing all the time. Like it's weird." Each time I drop Shiloh off to preschool, each push on the swing, each sticky handhold cherished by my warm hand, every time I set a fourth place at my dining table for a holiday, I have our donor family to thank. Words are never enough—they gave me the gift of a lifetime with my daughter.

Keep singing your fierce song little bird. Go to sleep tonight, and tomorrow, sing a little louder.

## The Gift of a Lifetime

Somewhere out in the great void, a mommy is not buying a birthday cake. She is not tying balloons to the backs of chairs. She is not inviting six little kindergarteners to share the day with her son. She is painfully aware of all of this.

So am I.

Today we celebrate the life that gave us more birthdays, and the best gift of all: a chance for a lifetime with our daughter.

We celebrate a mother, who, in her darkest moment, chose life for another child. She chose life so that something good could come out of something bad. She gave her little angel the legacy of a Hero to a family of four strangers.

This book is not about organ donation. This book is proof of its miracle. Pediatric transplants are hard because families that are in a position to donate are often caught off guard. Please discuss organ donation with your whole family. Know that it might not be you making the decision. When we signed *all four of us* up to be donors, we sent an email out to our extended family and friends. No one wants to make this decision, but the emergency department, the ICU, is not the place to make it.

This family, who are not putting out party favors today have become heroes to us. Every breath, every heartbeat is our parting gift.

God Bless those who choose LIFE, who choose LIGHT in the DARKNESS.

So in a way, this book IS about a change of heart. Whether you check that box on your license or not. This life is to be lived. Start it again today.

"I am in love with my version of us."

## Goodbye. And, Also, You Can Never Leave Me

How many people would you say that I've met in my lifetime? 100,000? More? And everyone who has met me has a different version of Hilary Thompson. The guy on the other end of the phone who felt my frustration deeply as I argued over another medication his insurance company denied, well, he likely doesn't much care for his version of Hilary Thompson. That woman whose groceries I bought as she cried by her three-year old, the best friend I had in third grade who I haven't seen in years, my incredibly generous and forgiving mother, the guy I rear-ended fifteen years ago, my elementary school principal, my teenage daughter—they all have different versions of me, yes?

If this is the case, then I have a question for you: Which version of me dies when I die? Where does my principal's memory of me go when I am gone?

The answer is, it remains. Left, in the dark, warm folds of the heart, or the dusty corners in a distant part of the mind. Everyone gets to keep their version of Hilary Thompson.

And if this is true, that means my Shiloh stays with me too. Her tender and sticky little chubby hand gripping mine near the playground as she scans the park for potential friends, her confessions to me about sneaking screen time for one last Elvis documentary, the nights I left the hospital with her crying "Mommy I wuv you fousands!" The version of her that stretched her hands out, scooping water from within the innertube, exclaiming to her cousin "This is the life, Wyatt!" The way she adored her big sister and longed for a little sister so much it made my uterus ache. The times when the medical trauma was in full force and she told me she longed to leave my house and live in a tall tower, and wouldn't give me the password. The way she swooned, sparkly-eyed for Elvis (who replaced her cousin Jack). That night long ago, when, while mad at me, she turned to her stuffy and stoically said "I guess it's just you and me, Peep. You and me against the world."

I've written down dozens of phrases from that 87-year-old child. I've savored handholds and firsts, and kissed owies and caught vomit, and listened while she cried about not wanting to go to Jesus yet. I rocked her to sleep until she was eight, and I could no longer carry her to bed, and I've rocked her to sleep several times anyway, since then. I've listened to her talk in her sleep night after night, after night, and I even heard her sing in her sleep once. Who does that?

My Shiloh does that. I am in love with my version of us.

I love my version of you, too, unknown reader. I see you reading by the hospital bed, perhaps quietly crying, perhaps your hard years are behind you and you look back on your journey with a stinging fondness.

Wherever you are, I'd encourage you to write your own story. Memorize your version of that precious child of yours. Make it your love song. See yourself how they see you—the heroine of the story. Choose to shine your light on the things you want to remember, let go of the things that aren't serving you. Notice the gold into those beautiful cracks of yours, Mama. That's kintsugi.

I see it clearly.

Our first family picture with all 4 of us. Cardiac ICU, October 2011

The view from here is breathtaking. Yellowstone, 2023

# Notes

www.ingramcontent.com/pod-product-compliance
Lightning Source LLC
Chambersburg PA
CBHW031511120626
46545CB00005B/1828